The Book of
SHEFFIELD PLATE

RARE COMPLETE SHEFFIELD PLATE REVOLVING SUPPER SERVICE C. 1820

The Book of
SHEFFIELD PLATE

by

SEYMOUR B. WYLER

with

ALL KNOWN MAKERS' MARKS
including
VICTORIAN PLATE INSIGNIA

PROFUSELY
ILLUSTRATED

❧

BONANZA BOOKS
NEW YORK

Contents

C. 6087814-2

To

My wife and three children

and

with the hope that my sons Michael and Richard will continue in this field of endeavor with which their respected grandfather, Sigmund Wyler, was associated since 1890.

This edition published by Bonanza Books,
a division of Crown Publishers, Inc.
A B C D E F G H

List of Illustrations

Note: All the illustrations, with the exception of the frontispiece, are contained in a Pictorial Section following page 84. The photographs are arranged according to articles shown, as follows:

Foreword

MY PURPOSE IN writing *The Book of Sheffield Plate* is to provide an interesting and readable guide for collectors and dealers who are seeking knowledge of both Sheffield Plating and electroplating. During the past thirty years both Sheffield and Victorian Plate have risen to amazing prominence. This is readily understandable—for a new collectors' field for those with limited means has been opened. In most cases the prices of specimen pieces of Sheffield Plate are still considerably less than comparable examples in solid silver, while Victorian Plated wares are often obtainable at just a fraction over the cost of good commercial plated ware.

Bradbury's *History of Old Sheffield Plate* was the first authentic and historic guide to the industry. Unfortunately, the book is now out of print and consequently of high cost. Inasmuch as no previous work on the subject of Victorian Plate has been published, I feel that the combined histories included in *The Book of Sheffield Plate* will provide a comprehensive reference work.

No effort has been spared to detail all pertinent data relative to both industries. All available information is included as to the methods employed both at the inception of the industry of Sheffield Plating and at its conclusion. I have discussed the innumerable craftsmen who are responsible for the craft's rise and acceptance in the field of art, because frequently in the absence of hallmarks, works of these men are recognized only by style. I have included every known means of identification, so that even the amateur collector will feel a sense of assurance in the recognition of an original. As a finale to the portion of the book devoted to Sheffield Plate, I have listed the most complete group of marks ever assembled as well as classification of the pieces made during the era.

Although for many years the silver plated products of the Victorian age were by-passed as merely secondhand and commonplace, they have finally achieved a rank of importance in the mind of today's prospective buyer. While it is true that during this prolific era much was undesirable, we have inherited countless examples that bear the stamp of fine workmanship. A detailed study has been included to assist the reader in distinguishing the wheat from the chaff.

SEYMOUR B. WYLER
New York, April, 1949

Chapter One

Definition of Sheffield Plate—
Discovery of the Process

❧

NO TERM IN THE world of art has been so misused as "Sheffield Plate." The title has become erroneously a common parent to all pieces consisting of a copper base plated with silver, while in truth it should apply only to those wares created by the process of fusion. Many misleading terms, such as "Real Sheffield," "Genuine Sheffield Plate" and just plain "Sheffield," are used when referring to modern electroplated articles. In a manner of speaking, the public at large is responsible for the use of these suggestive phrasings, for people have come to reject pieces termed "silver plated" as being common and undesirable. Nothing could be further from the truth, for a great deal of fine silver plate has been produced since early in the Victorian period. Innumerable authentic reproductions, as well as new creations, bear the stamp of fine workmanship and high quality.

The application of common sense with regard to many of the present-day offerings would immediately condemn them as spurious and impossible, for such articles as cigarette boxes, silent butlers and match boxes were non-existent during the nineteenth century. Yet, pieces such as these are offered daily to would-be purchasers, with the one-word description of "Sheffield." It is the main purpose of this work to stamp indelibly in the mind of the collector, the knowledge necessary to distinguish between originals and reproductions. Although the acquisition of these facts will of necessity result in great disappointment to many owners, it is far better to be well armed with the proper knowledge, for it will definitely prove a safeguard for further purchases.

3

If one would stop to consider that the life span of the industry of "Sheffield Plating" was less than a hundred years, during which the last sixty were the ones of productivity, it would be seen readily that all the thousands of articles sold as genuine could never have been produced. A perusal of the slow progress of the trade, plus a study of the many hardships that confronted its workers, will convince even the "doubting Thomases" that Sheffield Plate is rare and that not only the quantities but the creations themselves were very limited. Unfortunately, a lack of co-operation among dealers in old silver has caused an unbelievable amount of confusion in the minds of their clients, for in a reputable shop one is told the truth, while elsewhere the very factual statements here cited are vehemently refuted by those who are overanxious to consummate a sale.

It is the firm conviction of the author, based on many years of countless experiences with retail trade, that the old-silver dealer has slipped downward badly in the estimation of his clients. It is shameful, for the majority of those who are classified as proper merchants know beyond a doubt that businesses such as these can thrive only on confidence, and yet they suffer from ills beyond their control. Let the buying public be well armed with knowledge, for it is to them that we must appeal in order to eliminate those who are thriving illegitimately.

It is with this thought in mind that the author offers this history of one of the most fascinating trades in the annals of art. Through *The Book of Sheffield Plate,* which has been written as a companion to *The Book of Old Silver,* clear indisputable facts are presented, with the hope that they will hasten to break down the aura of mystery and skepticism that has too long been the bane of a greatly misjudged industry.

Although the discovery of Sheffield Plating, or the combining of silver with copper, was accidental, its importance in the history of manufacturing in England cannot lightly be discarded. The process derived its name from the city in which it was first produced, and so fantastic was its popularity that a poverty-stricken suburb of London soon grew to be one of the leading industrial centers of Great Britain.

Let us turn back the pages of history to a prosperous England in the year 1742, where the demand for luxuries was spreading to all classes. At this time, none but those of titled name or great wealth could afford those appointments which tended to create a little more gracious form of living. Primarily, the possession of silver was an expression of wealth, for the metal was scarce and the pieces made of it were costly. The raw metal was imported from India, which necessitated voyages of many months duration. Silversmiths were few in number and their wares in great demand, so it is not surprising that they were able to command high prices for their labors. Consequently, the ownership of family plate was confined to the rich, who gave little thought to what their indulgences might cost. Politically, the situation was such, that if they were short of funds, a direct appeal to the Crown would invariably result in higher land taxes to be paid to them, for this indeed was the main source of revenue for England's royalty. Yet, throughout this period wherein the demand far exceeded the supply, at no time did the silversmiths of Great Britain sacrifice the quality of their wares. Although we might not favor each piece that was executed, we cannot help but regard it with admiration for the fine ability that was ever-present.

A passing survey such as the foregoing will help one to understand better the immediate and popular reception that Sheffield Plate received. Basically, the ware resembled solid silver, and its lower cost enabled those of lesser income to enjoy for the first time the luxuries which had so long been denied to them. Essentially, plate was cheaper to produce than solid silver, for it contained a goodly proportion of copper as its base. However, this alone would not have made the great difference in price, for all metals in England were still scarce. Solid silver was heavily taxed, while articles of Sheffield Plate were not. The imposition of levies on luxuries was no new means of collecting additional funds for the English Crown, for throughout the history of the country we find evidence of this. However, no one paid much attention to the discovery of Sheffield Plating; many thought it only a passing fad and certainly not worthy of legislation. Twenty years later, when the industry had become firmly established, it was to be regarded in a new light and countless efforts were expended by leading silversmiths to impede its progress. By 1770, we shall see Sheffield Plate assume its rightful place in the world of art, and become a bone of great competitive contention to the trade of silversmithing.

The discovery of Sheffield Plating is accredited to one Thomas Boulsover in the year 1742. While employed in his occupation of a cutler, in the garret of a small building known as Tudor House, he was repairing the handle of a knife. He accidentally overheated the silver and copper in the haft, and found that at this temperature the two metals adhered. He tried to separate them, but found that a definite affinity had taken place. A further study of this phenomenon convinced Boulsover of the limitless possibilities of his discovery, and he was quick to take advantage of the knowledge. So was born the industry of Sheffield Plating, with its far-reaching effect.

Whether or not this is the actual story can be only a matter of supposition, for Boulsover kept scant records of his work. However, intensive research has led to the acceptance of this as the most probable of the stories of the discovery that we have inherited.

Being a man of vision, Boulsover found that his discovery could be turned into an advantageous business, and at the conclusion of a period of experimentation, he commenced the manufacture of buttons. These we have come to regard as the earliest examples of Sheffield Plate. He had soon built the production of buttons into a thriving trade, for they were far less expensive to make than their counterparts in solid silver, and there was a ready market to receive them. For several years he kept the process a secret, and for that reason had no opposition from rival tradesmen.

Although Boulsover was firmly convinced of the future possibilities of the business, he lacked the capital necessary to enlarge his plant for the production of buttons in quantity. He applied to a friend, Mr. Pegge of Beauchief, for the loan of seventy pounds. Mr. Pegge, who received him with extreme courtesy, lent him the money, and before twelve months had elapsed Thomas was able to repay the entire amount plus interest. This was done solely from the proceeds received from the manufacture of buttons; they were priced as high as a guinea a dozen, and the resulting profits were enormous.

Continued experiments with his new process enabled Boulsover to produce other articles, among the first of which were buckles and small boxes. His trade, however, was not purely a local one, and he was forced to employ a road salesman to travel to London and surrounding towns to contact new accounts. Unfortunately, the man engaged in this work was of dubious character, and fraudulently reported to Boulsover that there was no market for his wares. Actually, while in the plant he had carefully watched the new process and confided the means of its manufacture to a confederate in Sheffield. He turned over to his ally the many orders he received, and so discouraged Boulsover that he gave up this new business to devote himself to other enterprises. These included the manufacture of saws, to which industry he made many important contributions. It was indeed a sad blow to Boulsover, for the many others who followed him in the new trade found great wealth, while upon his retirement he was comparatively a poor man.

Although we have identified Boulsover as the discoverer of the process of Sheffield Plating, the furtherance of the industry is generally accredited to one Josiah Hancock. He was the first to realize the wide commercial possibilities of these new wares, and was the first craftsman to produce in Sheffield Plate household articles such as coffee pots and candlesticks. Many believe that Hancock learned the trade as an apprentice to Boulsover, but here again the records are rather incomplete. At any rate, he was certainly responsible for the growth and popularity of the new industry, and his many important contributions to it paved the way for the dozens of firms soon engaged in manufacturing by the new process. It is interesting to note here, that after fifteen years of production, Hancock gave up the making of finished pieces and devoted himself to supplying the trade with rolled metal. This took place sometime between the years 1762 and 1765.

The ability of man to combine metals certainly existed prior to the time of Boulsover, for we have inherited examples that date from the second and third centuries. Elaborate horse trappings which show evidence of silver plating on a base metal are known to have existed as early as the time of the Romans. In addition, specimens of unusual scabbards of swords and dagger hilts are known. Examples of Hebraic silver of plate composition used in the religious service of the temple have been unearthed, but the most careful study has failed to reveal the process of their manufacture. However, they are certainly the first attempts at silver plating, but it is feared an aura of mystery will forever enshroud them.

The instant popularity of Sheffield Plate was truly amazing, and we shall trace in the following pages not only the wide variance of pieces produced by the platers but the high degree of perfection they achieved in their work. It is not to be thought that every article made was of fine caliber, for many display definite evidence of lack of ability on the part of the craftsmen. Yet, one cannot help but admire the progress which

they registered in surmounting the great difficulties that they encountered. Improvements in the manufacture of pieces were the results of
hard labor plus the experience that many of the workers had gleaned in
silversmiths' shops. And a state of brotherhood existed between neigh-
boring and rival firms, wherein they constantly exchanged ideas for the
general good of the trade. Although but few new articles were introduced
which differed from those being made in solid silver, an unbelievable
amount of effort went into their production. Many times, pieces which
were finished were never marketed, for the masters felt they were unworthy. It is, perhaps, this pride in production plus the present-day
scarcity that accounts for the great number of collectors of Sheffield
Plate. Originals are eagerly sought after and, once gained, are treasured
with the respect due them. Their method of manufacture was indeed
unique, and it seems a pity that the life of the industry was so abruptly
terminated in 1838 by the discovery of electroplating.

We must ask the reader to view the history of plating with a keen
sense of imagination, for few records were kept during the early years,
and we will find that laws governing production were not invoked until
nearly thirty-five years after the discovery of the process.

Chapter Two

Laws Regulating the Production
of Sheffield Plate

❧

THE LAWS that governed the production of solid silver in England were far different from those that applied to plated articles. Perhaps the greatest amount of confusion in the mind of the layman is encountered by the absence of marks on Sheffield Plate, and it is for that reason that we shall devote considerable time to a full explanation of the various insignia found on silver and silver plated ware. It is a daily occurrence for a customer to walk into a shop today and inquire about a piece of Sheffield Plate, with the question, "Where are the hallmarks?" This query is a natural one, for the average person knows that silver is normally identified by the marks impressed on it. However, when the truthful response of a salesman confirms the lack of hallmarks on Sheffield Plated pieces, the customer is naturally bewildered. Most Sheffield Plate, we will discover, was unmarked. The reason for it is so obvious that a careful study of this chapter will clear up in the mind of the prospective buyer those perplexities that might have previously existed.

With the production of the first pieces of silver in England, it was recognized that some common standard of metallic content of a piece would have to be instituted, for without such a regulation no silversmith could honestly offer his endeavors as being genuine. The first mention of a Goldsmiths Company appears as early as the year 1180, but the association was purely voluntary, and carried little power. During the thirteenth century many silversmiths were quick to take advantage of the lack of regulations applied to their craft, and produced pieces of a far lower degree than the generally accepted standard used at that time.

This standard was the same as that used by the government for silver coinage; but inasmuch as the resulting pieces looked much the same, whether or not they contained a greater or lesser amount of alloy, the unscrupulous silversmiths saw an easy way to greater profits. During the fourteenth century the silversmiths formed an association which was called a Guild. Inasmuch as the meetings were held regularly in a local hall, the term hallmark was applied to the approved stamp upon which they had voted impressed on every piece of marketed silver. The word hallmark is a literal interpretation, for it was actually the mark of a Hall or Guild.

With the formation of the first Guild, a law of Parliament decreed that no silver could be smelted for purposes of manufacture unless it was first assayed and proved to contain the correct amount of silver and alloy. In 1335 another law was passed, which required each silversmith to punch on his wares a particular mark of his own, so that his work could be identified. It is interesting to note here that the earliest makers' marks were invariably in the form of an object such as an animal, flower, or household article. As the majority of the public was illiterate, the system of impressing one's initials was not instituted until the middle of the sixteenth century. Therefore, it is not incorrect to assume that if one finds a piece of silver with the insigne of a fish, the name of the silversmith was probably Fish. Unfortunately, the earliest makers' marks were not recorded with proper identification, and it is not until 1698 that we find the beginning of a complete category with actual names of silversmiths clearly established.

In 1477, the additional mark of a leopard's head was incorporated, to identify an article which had been properly assayed. Two years later the use of the date letter was inaugurated. This method of registering a year in which a piece was made has been invaluable, for in no country other than England, can one establish the exact year in which a piece was produced. As the trade flourished in London, a particular mark was assigned to pieces in this city, and with the establishment of Guilds in other centers of production, different town marks were introduced.

These insignia constitute what is known as a set of hallmarks, and all silver produced in England, up to and including that made today, is required by law to bear these marks. A further study of hallmarks on silver articles will show variations and deviations that took place throughout the years, but as we are concerned primarily with Sheffield Plate we shall not go into detail about these. The one exception, exempting pieces from being hallmarked, applied to any silver made for the Royal Family. Beyond that all pieces are marked. The Guild that regulated the use of these marks held great power and the goldsmiths' and silversmiths' organizations were held in high esteem, for the workers in this trade commanded the respect due great artisans. It was this pride in the work of the men who made up the industry that compelled the Guild to go to extreme measures to enforce the laws pertaining to the trade. Those workers who did not comply with the required regulations were heavily fined, and there are known cases where men were put to death for willful forgery of silver.

All the foregoing applied to pieces produced of solid silver, but the laws did not cover workers in Sheffield Plate. Actually, Sheffield Plated articles were never hallmarked, for at no time was there a regulated amount of silver and alloy required by law. The only insignia found were makers' marks and these were used purely for purposes of identification. Prior to the formation of the first Guild in the city of Sheffield in 1773, the makers of plate marketed their wares at their own will, with or without a sign of recognition. Those that adopted a maker's mark generally struck it three or four times in a row so that it might assume the look of the mark on a piece of solid silver. In addition, they partly obliterated these, so that it was practically impossible for a buyer to distinguish between a piece of silver and a piece of plate. The finished articles so resembled each other that only an expert could correctly distinguish the genuine silver from the Sheffield. This resulted in a very profitable business for those engaged in unscrupulous misrepresentation, for the plated articles could be produced for about one-fifth the price of their counterparts in solid silver. A further variation of the stamping of a maker's initials several times in a row was the use of a man's name as a central mark with his initials punched on either side.

As more and more Sheffield Plate appeared on the market, a rising wave of indignation among the silversmiths in London was evidenced, for they had come at last to recognize Sheffield Plating as a proper trade and one which was becoming injurious to their own business. At first the London Guild did everything in its power to hamper the production of the new wares, but this resulted in a sharp controversy with those living in Sheffield, for the industry was now bringing much prosperity to this former suburb. The silversmiths of Sheffield now banded together and requested the privilege of their own local Guild. They promised that they would regulate the trade and rule out the malpractice of forged marks. In the year 1773, the Guild was established in Sheffield, while at the same time the privilege was also granted to the town of Birmingham. In all probability the original idea of using marks to identify pieces of Sheffield Plate can be traced to the fact that many of the early plate makers were originally cutlers, and the laws that applied to the production of cutlery required proper marks of identification.

The Guild in Sheffield strove desperately to enforce legislation to correct the misdemeanors then existing, for the platers knew that without the friendship of the London houses they would lose a great part of their trade. The manufacturers in Sheffield of both silver and plate liberally supplied the London shops with much of the goods that were marketed there, and inasmuch as the great wealth existed in the capital, it was necessary to retain this friendship for the trade to prosper. The first law passed fixed a definite selling price for an article and limited the allowable discount to twenty percent for cash and fifteen percent for credit. In 1777, a further commission of ten percent was allowed for any person outside the trade who introduced a customer. The meetings of the Guild were attended with required regularity, with a fine imposed for nonattendance. However, the association was finally terminated in 1784.

It was with great difficulty that the silversmiths of Sheffield and Birmingham obtained their own assay offices, but their reasons for requesting it were sound; and much as the London Guild hated to yield any of its power, it could not help doing so. Primarily, the request was based on the fact that a great delay resulted from having to send the goods to London to be assayed. This was definitely true and resulted in the increased selling cost of an article to the extent that the provincial silversmiths claimed they could no longer produce pieces that would be competitive in price with those of their London brothers. The London Goldsmiths Hall denounced this application, charging their provincial rivals with fraudulent misrepresentation. In addition, they resented the use of what were now called pseudo-hallmarks, for they claimed they were used purely to confuse the public and were detrimental to the silver trade in general. (Evidence brought up during a discussion in the House of Commons clearly showed that the Sheffield platers had attained such a high degree of excellence in their work that it could scarcely be distinguished from solid silver.)

After much debate, permission was finally granted, with the understanding that the formation of the assay offices in Sheffield and Birmingham would be at the expense of the local silversmiths. However, the new Guilds were forced to incorporate a clause which absolutely prohibited the striking of any letter on any vessel of metal covered with silver. The penalty for infraction was a fine of one hundred pounds. During the next ten years, the Guild in Sheffield became so powerful that it was able to grant permission for a mark to be impressed on a plated vessel. Actually, the law permitted any manufacturer of plated goods in the city of Sheffield, or within a radius of one hundred miles, the right to impress on his wares his surname or corporate name together with a particular mark, figure, or device. However, it clearly stated that the insigne could not in any way imitate any known silver mark. And, further, these devices could be used only after proper registration at the Sheffield assay office. If approval were not granted, the penalty for the use of the mark was one hundred pounds.

Therefore, we now find that a manufacturer of plate was not required by law to stamp his wares, but might if he wished to do so, if the mark he used was a proper one. Very few manufacturers availed themselves of this privilege of registration. Between the years 1784 and 1836, the largest number recorded in any single year was nineteen, while several years showed a complete blank. The total number of marks recorded was one hundred and thirty-three; eighty being from Birmingham, fifty-two from Sheffield and one from London. It is well to mention here that the reason the Birmingham silversmiths registered at Sheffield was that the city was within the hundred-mile radius. Although the Birmingham workers complained, the law stood fast. Notwithstanding the fact that many more marks were registered from Birmingham, it is safe to assume that over seventy-five percent of the fused plate articles originated in Sheffield. The majority of Birmingham platers who registered were either jewelers, cutlers, or harness makers—with only a handful that could legitimately be described as manufacturers of Sheffield Plate.

A rather unusual situation developed during this period among the firms who produced both solid silver and Sheffield Plated articles. Having established makers' mark for their wares, they did not wish to lose this identification with the public and therefore, in defiance of the laws of the Sheffield Guild, they impressed the same makers' marks on both plated and silver pieces. Many of the pieces which were made by these manufacturers were sold only in London, and that is probably why this form of malpractice went unnoticed by the Sheffield Guardians.

In many cases, the shops in London who bought from these manufacturers insisted that the firm name be stamped on the piece, rather than the mark of the maker. It was difficult for the Sheffield platers to swallow their pride in order to obtain business. After having worked for many years to gain the privilege of registration, they had to forego its use in order to please their London clients. The direct result of this is noticed in many pieces which bear the name of a London shop properly impressed, with a set of initials directly below it. Inasmuch as the initials bear no relationship whatsoever to the retail firm, it is quite safe to assume that they were the identifying mark of the particular manufacturer in Sheffield. The only other marks found on Sheffield Plated pieces are numbers. These were manufacturers' recordings probably used for the purpose of assisting the retail shops in placing reorders. Unfortunately, many people misconstrue these numbers as being relative to a date, which leads to a great deal of unnecessary confusion.

The stringent laws and regulations under which Sheffield Plate was produced resulted in the omission of marks by nearly eighty-five percent of all those engaged in the industry. The Sheffield platers, generally speaking, had a ready market for their wares and for the most part did not bother to appear before the Guild to obtain registration. The assay office, however, did everything within its power to forestall the sale of any illegitimately marked piece, for it felt that public confidence was necessary if the factories were to produce at the fast pace that the industry was progressing. The average buyer of plated ware was of the middle class and consequently uneducated, and the Guild felt that if ugly rumors pertaining to its trade were voiced, irreparable harm would ensue. The Guild feared a lack of public confidence to such an extent that it assigned individual marks to those engaged in Sheffield Plating. These differed from those used by the manufacturers in the trades of cutlery making and close plating. The latter craftsmen were required to impress P S to denote plated steel, and B M to identify britannia metal. The

Guilds were taking no chances that these inferior products would be confused with genuine Sheffield Plate.

It should be clear at this point why so much Sheffield Plate is found unmarked. However, one must not look at an unmarked piece with disdain, for we have come to judge the examples of this period by their quality and style. Is it not reasonable to assume that although only fifteen percent of those engaged in the industry registered their marks, the other eighty-five percent would have been equally proficient and skilled? Those pieces made during the first twenty-five years of the industry which bear the pseudo-hallmarks are interesting from the standpoint of the collector. Not only are they desirable because of their early date, but also because they escaped destruction at the hands of the Guilds. It was common practice to obliterate forgeries in solid silver which came within the province of the Guilds, and one may assume that the same routine was followed with regard to Sheffield Plated pieces.

Again the author wishes to stress that all those pieces which may be offered to you bearing the various phrases "Genuine Sheffield," "Real Sheffield" and "Sheffield" are nothing but reproductions. It is far better to own an original without a maker's mark, than to acquire a piece with an improper tag of identification.

Chapter Three

The Problems of Manufacture and How They Were Overcome

❧

THE PROBLEMS that beset the manufacturers of the first articles in Sheffield Plate were undoubtedly more numerous than those with which they would normally be confronted today. The industry was in its infancy and each idea for production was nothing but an experiment which might or might not prove of value. In addition to this, the capital of most of these firms was very limited, and the metals which they used were costly. Consequently, it was to their advantage to waste as little as possible, for in many cases the misuse of basic materials might be responsible for a delay of several weeks. Whereas manufacturers in other industries had the opportunity to consult previous models, these early artisans had to work from imagination and conjecture.

The prime difficulty was the metal with which the craftsmen were dealing. Sheffield Plate consisted of a base of copper, coated with a layer of silver which would definitely wear off if put to hard usage. Although the popularity of Sheffield Plate at the time was caused by its close resemblance to solid silver, it is understandable that the market for it would drop immediately if pieces were not durable, even though its cost was so much less than the solid silver. The minute the silver wore off, exposing the base metal, the piece would be valueless to the buyer. In addition to this, there was the problem of ornamentation, and the application of attractive borders, for at all times the Sheffield platers were competing with a well-established production from their companion workers in solid silver. If the articles they produced were not equal in beauty, there might be no sales for them. We shall attempt merely to touch the high-

16

lights and give but a scant survey of these processes, for none but the most astute student would be interested in delving into the intricacies of the methods of production.

The most important problem was that of durability, and it is to the platers' credit that they finally surmounted this difficulty after many years of experimentation. Proof of this can be found in the many hundreds of fine Sheffield Plated articles that have survived the ravages of time, and are available in their original condition today. In the early days of Boulsover and Hancock, no definite proportion of the silver and copper content of an article was assigned in the manufacture of a piece. In the beginning, it was to a certain extent hit or miss, with no two articles being produced of exactly the same texture. It was only after many others had joined the trade and made their contributions that a general formula was adopted. Due to a lack of experience, the earliest platers deposited a very liberal thickness of silver, varying from ten to twelve ounces for each eight pounds of copper. This proportion, while it ensured durability, was costly, and for that reason, unsatisfactory, for it definitely removed the goods from a proper competitive level. It was not until about 1810 that the platers in general agreed on a proportion of five to seven ounces of silver for each eight pounds of copper. This was found to be a satisfactory ratio and the majority of pieces that we have inherited today were made from this formula.

About the year 1789, Samuel Roberts, one of the most proficient of the early platers, reached the pinnacle of his career as a manufacturer. He was determined to improve the quality of his product and alloted twenty-four ounces of silver to each eight pounds of copper. He called this "Bell Metal" because of his trademark of a bell. However, this proportion was of such great cost that he soon substituted a far lower silver content and joined other platers in the uniform ratio.

During the period between 1810 and 1815, we find the introduction of the rubbed-in silver shield. The popularity of Sheffield Plate had risen to such proportions by this time that much of it was finding its way into the homes of the nobility. Inasmuch as it was common practice for those of the gentility to exhibit their crests or coats of arms on all household silver, it was necessary to produce a product which would lend itself to engraving without damage to the piece. One finds many Sheffield Plated articles with a small surface in the center which seems to differ in color from the rest of the piece. This is known as a let-in silver shield, for actually this particular spot was made of solid silver. If you see an expert blow his breath on a piece of Sheffield it is in order to authenticate its age. For as the cloud of moisture disappears, the outline of the shield is clearly visible. Prior to the time of the introduction of these shields, it was not practical to engrave pieces, as the tools would cut through to the copper base and necessitate the replating of the article.

In studying the styles of Sheffield Plate, one would naturally assume that the earliest endeavors would have been severely simple, for to the layman it would appear that a smooth surface would be by far the least complicated to produce. However, this was not the case, for metal which is rolled and heated normally exhibits a series of ripples which are clearly visible to the naked eye. It was to cover up these deficiencies in quality that the earliest platers ornamented their work with chasing and repoussé work. However, these early examples reflect a definite lack of character and quality, for the Sheffield platers had not yet learned the intricacies of proper decoration. It was not until about 1789 that a fine type of engraving was introduced which was comparable in quality to the work of the leading silversmiths of the period. This led to the introduction of interesting and well-molded borders which had formerly been absent. About the year 1815, we find an outburst of decorative chasing in the form of heavily laden foliage and flowers. This was a reversion to the earliest type of embossing, but of a far superior character. Many collectors feel that these examples with the elaborately chased centers are the most desirable examples of the platers' art, for the quality of the work was excellent and the process of manufacture nearly perfect. Following the earliest years of production, the designs of Sheffield Plate were closely allied to those found on pieces of silver. Whenever a style had been popularly accepted, it was necessary to follow it in order to market the pieces successfully.

In collecting Sheffield Plate, one finds many examples that have been plated on only one side of the ingot. The unplated surfaces are usually the under surfaces of tea trays and salvers, as well as the insides of dish warmers and the bottoms of venison dishes and platters. This lack of plating had a double cause: not only did it contribute greatly toward the saving of costly material, but also the workers had not yet learned the art of plating on both sides of the base metal. With regard to the economical reason, the Sheffield smiths felt that those surfaces that were not exposed to the public eye need not carry the expense of silvering, and the consequent savings might be reflected in a more advantageous selling price. However, the absence of plate was never found on pieces which might be touched by edibles, for many felt that a certain metallic taste would be evidenced if the food made any contact with the copper. Occasionally, one finds examples from the early period silvered on the underneath side, but this process differed completely from that generally used. In these cases, two pieces of metal were laid back to back, only to ensure added strength, for the cost of this process was high. This method was rarely used, for it resulted in pieces far too heavy to be practical. Exemplary types are found in inkstands and trays.

Most of the early pieces showed little originality with regard to the design of borders, for it is here that the platers encountered their greatest difficulties. In 1785, the partnership of Roberts and Cadman introduced the solid silver edge. This was one of the most important contributions ever made to the industry of Sheffield Plating, for it enchanced the durability of the pieces at the points of hardest wear. The earliest borders were of thread, bead and gadroon design. About the year 1810, one finds the application of elaborate shell and scroll mounts as well as vintage and foliage motifs. These edges were applied in such a way that they soon became a distinguishing mark on Sheffield Plate. Today, many buyers look for this as a mark of antiquity, but here again we must warn that the presence of a solid silver rim is not a true test, for many reproductions are still made with this same type of border. These as a rule are evidences of willful misrepresentation.

The last of the difficulties encountered by the producers of Sheffield was the use of gold plating. The fanastic cost of gold and its high melting point, which incurred tremendous risks of manufacture, deterred workers from attempting to gild pieces. If a client demanded that this be done, it was usually executed at his or her risk, with no estimate given for the work until it had been completed. Generally speaking, the only pieces which showed the presence of gold plating were the insides of salt dishes and mustard pots. The reason for its use in these pieces was one of necessity, for if the condiments came in contact with the metal their erosive qualities would produce black spots. This reaction is not evidenced on gold, and in those pieces where glass linings were not available the platers used this method of protection. From the standpoint of cleanliness it was indeed desirable to gild the insides of many pieces, such as mugs, water pitchers and sugar bowls, but, unfortunately, few makers were sufficiently proficient at it. Throughout the industry one finds gilding used as a matter of expediency rather than for purposes of beauty. The two types used were fire gilding and mercury gilding, both of which possessed extreme qualities of durability.

It is truly amazing that the types of articles produced in Sheffield Plate were so varied. There was practically no original effort made in solid silver that was not at sometime or other produced in plate. This is indeed surprising when one considers the short duration of the industry. Every difficulty of production seems to have been surmounted by the platers and there was a constant rivalry which existed between the manufacturers of solid silver and Sheffield Plate. If, in a particular year, epergnes in solid silver were the fashion, one can rest assured that before much time had elapsed they were available in Sheffield Plate. By the year 1800, the workers had become so proficient that they were able to execute special orders which copied in detail the services made in solid silver. It was this ability, plus the low cost of Sheffield Plate as compared with silver, that caused the industry to rise to such great heights. However, if one considers that many of the firms who produced solid silver were also engaged in the production of plate, the style and production parallels of the two fields are not too remarkable. In many instances where a firm had made a special die for an article to be produced in solid silver, it was found indeed to be a very profitable business to reproduce many of the same in the lower price field. It was this production of similar pieces made in both metals that has led to the erroneous attribution of many designs as being original with the Sheffield Plate makers.

Chapter Four

Other Countries Where Sheffield Plate
Was Produced

❦

ALTHOUGH SHEFFIELD PLATE has always been identified with England, similar wares were produced elsewhere. However, the particular method of plating discovered by Boulsover was rarely used outside of Great Britain. Other procedures of manufacture are known to have existed throughout the Continent, but it is perhaps the fact that the worker in Sheffield carefully hoarded the secret of his process that prevented others from copying his methods. Regardless of construction, all of these efforts are included in the category of Sheffield Plate.

The combining of silver with a base metal, which is the primary function of any plated ware, is known to have existed as early as the days of the Egyptians. However, the methods which they employed are far too obscure to enable us to dismantle their work and discover how the ingredients were combined. A few centuries later, we find evidence of other plated goods wherein silver was combined with another metal, but the exact process of manufacture is again unknown. However, it is safe to assume that plating by fusion was never known prior to 1742, the year in which it was discovered by Thomas Boulsover. Although many contributions and improvements are noted throughout the short history of the industry, it is an undeniable monument to its discoverer that the original method he perfected was never changed.

The growing popularity of Sheffield Plated articles in the leading cities of England quite naturally led to their eventual discovery by surrounding countries. Sheffield Plate afforded the opportunity to both the Irish and Scotch to indulge their taste for luxury at a price they could afford.

As we have noted before, Sheffield Plated articles were about one-fifth the cost of their counterparts in solid silver, although this ratio would vary with reference to large weighty pieces, such as dinner services and table decorations. We shall deal primarily with Sheffield Plate in Scotland, Ireland, France, and the Continent, and then proceed to North America.

Sheffield Plate in Scotland

A most diligent search through the records of the cities of Edinburgh and Glasgow has not revealed any information indicating the existence of the Sheffeld Plate industry in Scotland. According to our accepted standard of the Scotsman as one of a nation of thrift-loving people, this is hard to believe. There were perhaps isolated makers who may have started life as apprentices in Sheffield, and produced bits at random, but the actual founding of a manufactory was unknown. However, one must not assume that a great quantity of Sheffield Plate was not purchased by the Scottish people, for records of the larger Sheffield firms of the time list sizeable exports of plated goods to the leading jewelers in Scotland. In order to establish a factory properly, a great deal of capital would have been required, and the enthusiasm necessary to venture into an important project such as this was always lacking. That was probably due to the fear that it would be impossible to compete with those firms who were now so well rooted in England. This was undoubtedly a lack of foresight on the part of those who might have financed the new trade, for in no other country could more success have been reaped than in Scotland. The people were thrifty, and they were industrious; and the majority enjoyed the benefits of hard labor, so that they had the wealth necessary to indulge themselves in the luxuries of good living. Always bearing in mind that to the naked eye Sheffield Plate and solid silver were very similar, is it not strange that an industry that fairly preached economy did not find a proper home here? The records of the two leading cities listed certain workers as being engaged in the industry of plating, but it is safe to assume that their association was with the trades of coach making, harness making, and ironmongering rather than with the trade as we know it.

Sheffield Plate in Ireland

We have inherited no evidence that Sheffield Plate was ever produced in Ireland, although the Royal Dublin Society did everything within its power to encourage the formation of a trade in this city. They felt that great savings would result from the founding of a manufactory at home, for not only would it be cheaper to produce the goods at a lower labor cost, but they could also save the expense of transportation.

In spite of the fact that there was considerable demand for Sheffield Plate in Ireland, there was little response from those engaged in the trade of silversmithing to venture into the new business. The records show that only one silversmith, John Lloyd, produced any plated goods at all. While the City Directories of both Dublin and Cork mention silver platers among those actively engaged in business at the time, it is probable that they were either in the retail business, in shops which marketed the wares of the English smiths, or else were representatives of makers of buttons and harness fittings. It is indeed strange that the industry did not flourish in Dublin, for at this time the people lived on a scale comparable to the Londoners, and at all times evidenced a keen appreciation of goods of high quality and style. This may be seen by viewing the work of the Irish silversmiths, who made many important contributions to the trade both in the production of new pieces and in the creation of unusually elaborate embossings peculiar to local wares.

The style of silver popular in Ireland was very different from that in England, and for that reason, one still finds today in Eire examples of Sheffield Plate that were made especially for export. These bear no resemblance at all to the domestic goods produced in Sheffield. A close study of Irish silver evidences the Irish preference for the ornate and many pieces bear chasing depicting the farm life so dearly loved by the people.

In years to come, as Ireland became a poorer and poorer country, a definite falling off of the trade with England was noted. At no time in the history of the country did it ever house a plant that produced silver plate. Perhaps a more determining factor was that at no time did the industry enjoy Royal patronage or protective duties. Those in control agreed that it would be impractical to try to establish a factory in Dublin that could successfully compete with those in England. The noticeable lack of apprentices in Ireland contributed to the absence of the trade, for those who were successful in the city of Sheffield felt it would indeed be a poor risk to expend their efforts in a locale where the reception seemed dubious. However, between the years 1790 and 1820 a great deal of Sheffield Plate was imported into Ireland, for plate represented the means whereby those who appreciated fine things and yet could not afford high luxury might indulge themselves. Unfortunately, most of the plate imported from England has disappeared and today it is indeed a rare occurrence to find a fine example in an Irish home. Undoubtedly, the high price commanded in the last forty years for specimen pieces of Sheffield Plate made it extremely profitable for those in Ireland who still owned it to dispose of their holdings.

Sheffield Plate in France

France was the only other country in the world that produced enough Sheffield Plate to warrant consideration as an industry. However, at no time was the work comparable to the degree of excellence attained by the manufacturers in Sheffield, nor was an extensive amount produced. There was much demand for Sheffield Plate, particularly in the larger cities, for the French by and large were a people who lived well. The example of indulgent living set for them by the Court soon became contagious.

While France was the largest customer in the importation of Sheffield Plate, the styles which were popular in Paris differed greatly from those wanted at home, and for that reason many firms created pieces especially for the foreign market. In particular, we note the firm of Roberts and Cadman, which formed a considerable business association with both France and Spain. However, the advent of the French Revolution in 1789 brought trade to a virtual standstill. France was so beset with internal trouble that there was a falling off of all exports, with the exception of munitions. With the decline of the French business, the many firms actively engaged in production in Sheffield were forced to look for new fields, for the business they had developed was a considerable one, and the loss of a customer such as France was sorely felt. Had it not been for the demand for goods from the English colonies at this time, it is doubtful whether many of the firms would have survived the crisis. It is interesting to note that with reference to all export trade with foreign countries, the businesses that were developed were eventually stifled. Perhaps the main reason for this decline was the high protective tariff which had already begun to be built up by countries abroad.

The method of plating in France differed greatly from that developed in England, as noted in the following survey. The French procedure was as follows: After a piece had been created, a very thin leaf of pure silver was applied. The article itself was never heated, but the temperature of the leaf was raised to such a high degree that it adhered to the base metal. The applied leaf was then burnished by pressure until it completely covered the surface being worked on. The process was a simple one, and only in the application of burnishing was extreme care necessary. However, the work was not practical for the covering of large areas of base metal, for an unbelievable amount of patience was required. Its important contribution—recognized by all workers in Sheffield Plate —was that the French method was most effective in repair work, for by this procedure an article that showed wear in a single part could be mended easily. This method of application of the silver leaf to a worn spot was in use for many years, even after the introduction of electroplating. It is readily understandable, if one visualizes the method used, that no simpler way could be devised than to cover the single bare patch with a foil of silver and in that way obviate the need for replating. However, this was not practical when applied to the borders of pieces or the nozzles of candlesticks, for in those instances where an undue amount of friction occurred, the hard wear was too great and caused the destruction of the leaf. In addition, the French method was not used for the purpose of introducing the silver shield, for the tool of an engraver might easily dislodge an entire silver leaf, and thereby spoil a whole piece.

It is not until 1772 that we find the founding of a factory in France wherein the principles of Boulsover's discovery were applied. This plant was under Royal patronage and for many years enjoyed a lucrative business which was financed by the French Court. The establishment was headed by Monsieur Degournay, an engineer in the employ of the King of France, and continued successfully until the middle of the nineteenth century. However, this new manufactory in Paris caused much dissension on the part of the French silversmiths, and in 1773 they sent a note of protest against the production of this class of merchandise. The result of their protest was completely unexpected, and did little more than bring added recognition to French Plate, to such an extent that before long King Louis XVI created a factory of his own.

The King knew that the very expensive solid silverware then in vogue could never be indulged in by the French middle classes, and he felt assured that a factory under Royal patronage would provide good-looking household table silver within the reach of those who aspired to it. The firm flourished to such an extent that the King allowed it to title the plate as being of the "Royal Manufacture." This so infuriated the Goldsmiths Company of England that they sent a protest to the "Court des Monnaies," but to little avail. Again a contrary effort was achieved by the protest, for through the King's influence, the firm was not only granted permission to continue with the production of Sheffield Plate wares, but also to gild and brass plate any base metals for household use.

The life of the industry in France was a short one, and soon after the introduction of electroplating in 1838, was terminated. During its existence, a few firms were outstanding as manufacturers of Sheffield Plate. Balaine, Durand, Levant and Gandias were leaders in the field, and it is not uncommon to find pieces created by these craftsmen for sale today. However, there was a decided difference in the look of a piece of fused plate as compared to a piece of French manufacture, for the French method seems to have resulted in a grayer finish and a lack of the patina usually found on English pieces.

The markings found on plate made in France varied greatly from those used in England, as a fairly complete mark of identification was required. In most cases, the name of the maker was impressed along with either the word "Doublé" or "Plaqué." In addition to this, it was obligatory to denote the thickness of the silver by a further mark, in order to show the relationship between the amount of silver and the amount of copper contained in the piece. Those which bear the highest numerals are indicative of the poorest quality, for the number which was struck signified the number of kilos of copper contained in respect to one kilo of silver.

The study of French Plate is an interesting one; and the acquisition of specimens, a worthy task. Unfortunately, much of the early plate was destroyed along with the beautiful examples of solid silver; for in times of hardship the French Court looked to those creations by the silversmiths, in order to reclaim sorely needed essential metals. As recently as the Second World War, this procedure was invoked in many countries throughout Europe, for at a time when copper was at a premium, it was found to be most expedient to resmelt such articles as heavy tea trays and platters for the base metal they contained.

If one is a collector of Sheffield Plate, it would indeed be advisable to include several specimens of the French platers' art, for they show extreme differences side by side with the work of the English craftsmen of the period.

Sheffield Plate on the Continent

Although several countries were known to have carried on an importing trade with the platers in Sheffield, at no time did the ware become popular. It was perhaps because Sheffield did not represent in their minds a genuine article, but rather a poor imitation of the real. This feeling is true even today, and anyone engaged in the silversmith trade easily recognizes the difficulties of selling plated ware, old or new, to those from foreign lands. Spain, Italy, Germany, Holland and Russia are known to have traded on a limited scale, but the substance of it was so small that it is barely worth mentioning.

However, it is safe to assume that travelers from foreign lands, who may have visited England, brought back pieces of Sheffield Plate with them. This is evidenced by the discovery every once in a while, of a piece of plate in a country thousands of miles from Great Britain. It is questionable whether any Sheffield Plate was produced in these countries, although certain pieces that have come within our ken would indicate that isolated workers attempted some efforts in this direction. Pieces with the mark of a spread eagle, similar to that found in the crests of German and Austrian nobility, are known, and for that reason we may assume that their place of manufacture was in one of the Teutonic countries. It is a matter of record that a mark such as this was never used by any English smith. Other examples of foreign plate have been noted in pieces wherein the makers' marks have been struck in Russian and Italian. Here again, it can only be assumed that isolated silversmiths with a bit of spare time on their hands may have turned their skills to producing Sheffield Plate. In all probability, judging from the styles of the pieces noted, they attempted to reproduce articles which may have been brought back by travelers. Therefore, let us state definitely that, to the best of our knowledge, no actual factories actively engaged in the production of Sheffield Plate are known to have existed in the eighteenth century outside of England and France.

Sheffield Plate in North America

As early as 1795, England was engaged in a very prosperous trade with the New World. Many luxuries which had heretofore been confined within the boundaries of Great Britain were slowly finding new homes on the shores of North America. America was a young country, but a rich one, populated mainly by those who had left England not too many years previously. Many of these early colonists were of good families and great wealth, and their love for fine things was easily indulged. It is evident that the great number of artisans who were busily engaged at their trade in this period had more than enough work at their benches to keep them busy for years to come. Therefore, the silversmiths had no time to bother about the new process, due to the fact that the demand for real silver was so great. Actually, not one piece of Sheffield Plate of American manufacture has come to light.

Among the silversmiths in America were many who had fled persecution. The ideas that they brought with them, plus the experience which they had gained in both England and the Continent, resulted in a great demand for the fine type of silver that was then being produced in America, in addition to the solid silver that was being imported. Had the Sheffield Plate industry continued after 1840, there is little doubt that many factories would have been founded, for the American people took eagerly to the luxury of silver as representing an expression of wealth in their homes.

The tendency to copy from the English was quite apparent and can be noted in all the expressions of artistic efforts in the New World.

With regard to Canada, it appears that Sheffield Plate found no popularity there, for only one firm imported it, and that to the value of less than a hundred pounds. No workers were engaged in the manufacture of plate in that country.

Chapter Five

Outstanding Makers of Sheffield Plate

⚜

ALTHOUGH HUNDREDS of workers were engaged in the industry of Sheffield Plating, due to a lack of registration we are able to identify only a handful. Only fifteen percent of the workers availed themselves of the opportunity of using the maker's mark, and for this reason but few names can be listed among the leading artisans. There must have been dozens more who made important contributions to the industry, but their work can be recognized merely as a style, rather than identified with a particular individual. We shall deal with the life histories of only seven or eight, but these few are known to have fostered the industry and been responsible for the wonderful appreciation which followed in the wake of their best efforts.

Throughout the history of art, one always finds certain craftsmen whose creative genius has lifted them far above the rank and file of their competitors, and it is to these that the world has paid homage for centuries. The signature of an artist on a picture may identify it immediately as a specific work of the person in question whereas in the production of a piece of silver or Sheffield an entirely different viewpoint must be taken. Normally the hallmarks on a piece of silver will identify it as the work of a particular firm to which full credit is given for its manufacture. However, it is entirely possible that a dozen craftsmen and apprentices may have contributed their particular skills in the production of the finished piece. For example, one might take a tea service which was first sketched by an artist who had in mind a distinctive style and design. When the decision was reached to produce this piece, many hands were busily engaged in various forms of silversmithing before the article was completed. These might include an engraver, a hammer man, a solderer and a burnisher. Yet the names of these contributors are never brought to light and appreciation is given only to the firm whose maker's mark is indelibly impressed on the service. It is, therefore, a little unfair to single out less than a dozen men and give them the full credit for the high degree of excellence attained by the Sheffield platers. However, it was probably the consummation of their ideas, plus a certain knowledge, that resulted in the high quality of the pieces produced. It is for this reason that we owe a definite debt to the following men whose work throughout the history of the industry was typical of the best.

Thomas Boulsover

Naturally, the first name to be recognized in the annals of Sheffield Plate is that of Thomas Boulsover, who was born in 1704 and died at Whiteley Wood Hall in 1788. It was through his discovery of the method of combining metals that the world inherited Sheffield Plate, and it indeed seems unfortunate that he gained so little materially from the trade. Doubtless it was his unsuspecting nature that brought him such little monetary consideration. For he permitted other workers to copy from his trade secrets and market their wares unmolested. Had he been a more astute businessman he would undoubtedly have been able to retire with ample funds at an early age. As the inventor of a new product, he was justly entitled to the royalties which were never paid to him.

Josiah Hancock

Josiah Hancock has always been associated with the trade of Sheffield Plating, for to the best of our knowledge he did more to foster the industry at the time of its infancy than any other single worker. While great respect has been paid to his outstanding ability, he has never been accurately identified. The name Hancock was widespread in the city of Sheffield and many families of that name were associated with the trade of metal smithing. Just who this particular Josiah Hancock was is a matter for conjecture, for unfortunately the records were never very clear in regard to his career. The generally accepted story is that he was born about the year 1711 and at the age of fourteen was apprenticed to the trade. Sometime during the following few years he was employed by Thomas Boulsover and it is clearly during this period that he learned so much of the intricacies of working with metals. Directly after the discovery of the method by Boulsover, it is to Hancock's credit that he alone foresaw the tremendous possibilities in the process. Much is made of one Josiah Hancock who in 1764 was listed as a master cutler and he probably is the same man who was associated with the manufacture of Sheffield Plate. No greater respect could be paid to his ability than was written in his obituary in 1791 wherein he was called "The Father of Silver Plate Manufacturers." During his lifetime he was chosen as one of the thirty original Guardians of the assay office in Sheffield and was elected a life member of the town's trusteeship.

As early as the year 1758, the name of Hancock began to be identified with the industry. Pieces bearing his maker's mark were seen in many of the leading shops. He, at this time, was the outstanding craftsman, and comparison with contemporary workers will prove this beyond a doubt. His work showed a style similar to that of the great silversmiths, and his inherent ability to overcome the obstacles which beset most workers in the trade was easily noticeable. Many who have studied the history of Sheffield Plating feel that Hancock should share the fame given to Boulsover, for although Boulsover discovered the process of plating it was turned into a proper industry under the guidance of Josiah Hancock. The term "rediscoverer" was often applied to Hancock, for many felt that by 1758 Boulsover had discarded his discovery and returned to other industries while Hancock was constantly improving production methods. A life history of Hancock by Dixon credits him with being the first person to make any practical improvements in the industry. It is said that his ability and contributions to the manufacture of plate removed many coworkers from the lowly depths of button making to the high plane enjoyed by leading silversmiths. The method of plating on both sides of the ingot was perfected by Hancock. This contribution alone opened the path for the hundreds of household articles that were made by later craftsmen. It permitted for the first time the making of domestic plate, both sides of which were well executed. It is said that leading silversmiths studied the work of Hancock and improved pieces made for their own trade.

Tudor and Leader

Men like Boulsover and Hancock worked as individuals and the result of their efforts can honestly be associated with their particular abilities. It was not until the formation of a partnership by Henry Tudor and Thomas Leader that an actual factory for the production of Sheffield Plate was instituted. The association formed by these two men was most agreeable and profitable. Thomas Leader came to Sheffield after having served an apprenticeship in a London silvershop where he gained great experience. His contributions to the trade were many and the factory created by these two men permitted for the first time the production of pieces on a large scale. Prior to the opening of the factory the two men were faced with the necessity of raising a considerable amount of capital, for the cost of tools and machinery was great. A Doctor Sherburn, a local Sheffield man, foresaw the possibilities and financed it from its inception. Before many years had passed his foresight was well repaid, for Tudor and Leader became the largest and most notable plate makers in the city. Later, another member of the Leader family joined the firm and in 1783 Samuel Nicholson was given a partnership. At this time the name of the firm was changed to Tudor, Leader and Nicholson and was registered under the name of Tudor and Company. Upon the retirement of the two original members, the formation of two new companies is noted, one being under the guidance of Tudor and Nicholson and the other an association of the two Leaders, Daniel and Thomas, Jr. Eventually the firm of Tudor and Company was taken over by John Round and Sons and parts of the original plant may still be seen today in what was then called Sycamore Hill.

Thomas Law

Another instance of a cutler who eventually turned to the trade of Sheffield Plating is found in that of Thomas Law. Born in 1717, he was an apprentice to the Cutlers Company in 1730 and registered as a master in 1753. At this time he turned to the new trade and for twenty years prior to his death produced many pieces of high quality bearing his individual maker's mark of a squatty vase. A son, John Law, carried on the trade until 1828 when the firm was taken over by Law, Atkin and

Oxley. This original firm is still in business today at the Truro Works in Sheffield under the name of Atkin Brothers.

Thomas Bradbury

The only family still in business today that can trace an unending association with the trade of Sheffield Plating is that of Bradbury. The original member of the family actively engaged in the industry was Joseph, who was apprenticed in 1750 and admitted as a freeman of the Cutlers Company in 1760. Thomas, the son of Joseph, entered the trade at an early age and was apprenticed to Matthew Fenton and Company in 1777 when he had reached his fourteenth birthday. After eight years with this firm he entered into an agreement to teach the trade to John Fenton, the son of the original founder of the firm. Upon the death of the elder Fenton in 1795 the business was sold to Thomas Watson and Bradbury, formerly Thomas Watson and Company. Each succeeding son of the Bradburys was an apprentice to the trade. In 1832 the factory was moved to the corner of Arundel Street and was actively engaged in the manufacture of silver and plate up until a few years ago. At the time of the retirement of Frederick Bradbury, the original dies were sold to Atkin Brothers. Although the firm of Watson registered a mark for plate goods about 1795, few marked examples are found, for they rarely used it.

At this time the author would like to pay the greatest respect to Frederick Bradbury, who in 1912 published his outstanding work, *The History of Old Sheffield Plate*. Its pages reveal the almost unbelievable amount of time and effort he spent on it. Incidentally, it was the first history of Sheffield Plate ever written.

Samuel Roberts

At least two families by the name of Roberts were actively engaged in Sheffield Plating during the latter part of the eighteenth century. The company with whom we are primarily concerned was the one formed by the two brothers, Jacob and Samuel. This firm was originally identified with the cutlers' trade and for many years was outstanding as manufacturers of table knives. Many branches of the family were actively associated with the trade, but it is to the son of the original Samuel Roberts that the highest honors must be paid for his worthy improvements. Shortly after Samuel, Jr., had served his apprenticeship, his father built a factory for him and in May, 1784 the business was begun. The young Roberts showed a remarkable aptitude for the trade plus a keen business insight. He was the first to introduce silver borders, stamped silver-filled feet, handles and mounts as well as bright cut engraving. The process of a rubbed-in silver shield is also attributed to him. Between the years 1785 and 1810 he was far and away the outstanding maker of Sheffield Plate and his work is compared to that of Matthew Boulton. He is responsible for the invention of the telescopic candlestick in 1798, the folding toast rack and a special process for plating on white metal. Shortly before the introduction of electroplating he began using German silver as a base. In addition to being the head of one of the most successful firms in Sheffield, Samuel Roberts devoted much time to benevolent activities and public life. He was the author of several books as well as a constant contributor to the local newspapers. Unfortunately, he expended most of his energy and enthusiasm during the first twenty-five years of his association with the trade. As he advanced in years his ability waned and his later examples are not to be compared with his early efforts.

Thomas Nicholson

Thomas Nicholson was born in 1779, the son of Samuel, formerly a partner in Messrs. Tudor and Leader. He lived until 1860 and his career was unique in that he was associated with the trade not only during the time of plating by fusion but for twenty years after the introduction of electroplating. As early as the age of six, he evinced an unusual interest in designing and was allowed the run of the factory with which Samuel Roberts, Sr., was associated. During these first years he made many crude drawings in his copy book, and prior to his teen age showed great aptitude for the trade. Nicholson is responsible for many intricate and unusual decorations used on Sheffield Plate shortly after 1800. It was he who first designed the motifs of dolphins and shells worked into the gadroon border. This new fashion completely revolutionized the former stereotyped styles. This design grew in popularity, for the people had begun to tire of the severely plain pieces which were then the vogue. His influence in the new type of border was so widespread that many London silversmiths were compelled to include the design in their works. Great difficulty was encountered by the makers of solid silver in the manufacturing of these borders, for where the Sheffield workers relied on the use of dies, the silversmiths had to mold and cast special forms incorporating these flower decorations. This instance is but one proof wherein the Sheffield makers created designs which were later copied by the silversmiths.

Throughout his entire career Nicholson was a creative genius; and it was he who was responsible for many of the unusual Arabesque motifs, in addition to the use of leaves and flowers instead of reeded borders. In his diary he recorded many interesting facts regarding the trade in general and spoke of alternating periods of success and depression experienced by the makers of plate. In his opinion, a magnificent opportunity for exporting plate to the Continent was missed, for the Foreign Office rejected all applications for representation in foreign lands. At one time in his career he was associated with a man by the name of Gainsford, but this partnership terminated shortly after the introduction of electroplate. He showed keen interest in the new process discovered by Elkington and joined the firm of James Dixon, which was outstanding in the production of electroplated wares.

Matthew Boulton

Matthew Boulton was a most gifted individual, who contributed many ideas which were world-wide in effect. Both his ability in the field of art and his mechanical aptitude were of the highest degree. Here indeed was a man who was doubly blessed—with an inventive mind and a personality that made him beloved by all who knew him. In the entire history of the city of Birmingham there has been no other individual who contributed more toward making it one of England's leading industrial centers.

Boulton was born on September 3, 1728 in Birmingham. At this time his father had a well-established business of toy making which included the production of buckles. Matthew left school at the age of fourteen to enter his father's business, and he was entrusted with the entire management by the time he was twenty-one years old. What further proof of his business acumen could be found than that this great responsibility was given to a mere lad who had barely outgrown his teens? However, his father was an intelligent man who immediately saw that Matthew's capacity for leadership was not to be denied and felt that if he were given a free rein he would do everything to forge ahead successfully. In addition to his large business interests, Boulton led an active social life and married at an early age. Unfortunately, his wife died about four years after the marriage and within another year his father passed away.

Boulton was the type that needed companionship of a woman and about 1767 he secretly married the younger sister of his late wife. Although this was contrary to the law of the church to which he belonged, he received the blessing of his mother-in-law. This union resulted in his receiving a rather large inheritance which, had he been of a less ambitious nature, would have provided for his retirement from business in comparative comfort. However, the life of a country gentleman had no appeal for him. He regarded the money he inherited as rather the means by which he could expand and enlarge his business. A sidelight on his social life is interesting, for through mutual friends Boulton was privileged to meet Benjamin Franklin, and the two became fast friends. Many interesting letters have been preserved which proved not only the depth of their friendship but showed the exchange of intellectual ideas between individuals of the highest inventive capacity.

Having heard of the remarkable rise of the Sheffield Plate industry, Boulton went to Sheffield to acquaint himself with the technique of the process. In 1762 he successfully introduced its manufacture in a district called Soho. It was beyond a doubt the only factory outside the city of Sheffield that produced the new ware for at least the next twenty-five years. As Boulton's business increased, he clearly saw that one large manufactory to house a great number of workmen would result in better production at a far lower cost. With this in mind, he formed a partnership in 1762 with John Fothergill, who was primarily a merchant with good connections in the foreign markets. Although this association did not last long, it offered Matthew considerably more time to devote himself to the mechanics of the business, for Fothergill took charge of the selling. As the business in the Soho plant increased, Boulton became the largest single manufacturer of Sheffield Plate of the period. Yet at no time were the goods produced in such a way as to lessen their quality in order to meet competition. Rather let it be said that the pieces which came from the Boulton factory were the finest the world has ever known, and rarely in the future were they ever equalled for quality and beauty. Although

Boulton made but few contributions to the industry, he studied every improvement going on about him at the time and this led to the production of only the best in Sheffield Plate. Unfortunately, he never registered his famous mark of a double sunburst until 1805, so it is impossible to identify him accurately with hundreds of pieces that were almost surely the result of his handiwork.

It is a notable tribute to his over-all enthusiasm that while he devoted the major portion of his time to the new work at Soho, he did not neglect his father's large plant. He increased the business and introduced the manufacture of steel jewelry which included not only buckles but ornamental neckclasps, watch chains and chatelaines, all of which were the height of fashion at the time. In addition to the factory plus the Sheffield Plating plant, Boulton interested himself in the production of Ormolu which was the French name for an amalgam consisting of gold which had been finely ground up with mercury. Its primary use was in gilding ornamental brass and household objects. It enjoyed its greatest popularity in France where the taste for the rococo was ever in vogue. At another period of his life, Matthew evinced great interest in the manufacturing of pottery and nearly engaged in a partnership with his good friend Josiah Wedgwood, who had just started his new works at Etruria. Unfortunately, he did not continue along these lines, or else the world might have inherited magnificent pottery bearing his trade-mark. He merely dabbled in the business in a small way wherein he mounted pieces of Wedgwood in Sheffield fittings.

Boulton's desire to create masterpieces in Sheffield and Ormolu led him further afield than contemporaries who were content merely to produce general household wares. His wish to copy from the masterpieces of other generations was so fervent he employed a special buyer to travel on the Continent in order to secure rare originals in other lines of art. He spent a great deal of time both in the salesrooms at Christie's and in the museums. Unfortunately, the laws that governed museums were such that no person was admitted without written permission and at no time were more than five persons allowed to remain at the same time. Another interesting sidelight of this curious law was the provision that limited the visiting time to one hour. However, Boulton appealed to those in power and secured very special grace which permitted him countless hours wherein he studied the great masterpieces housed by the galleries.

Many of these were later reproduced by him. Naturally, Boulton was little interested in retaining these art objects after they had been copied and it is just another tribute to his keen business ability that most of the things which he resold at auction earned a profit. His wanderings in the world of art soon turned his interest to the manufacturing of clocks, and there is definite evidence to prove that he produced several between the years 1769 and 1772. However, this is one of the few enterprises into which he entered wherein he did not meet with great success.

His fame had spread far afield and before long he was called into consultation by the Adam brothers, who were at the height of their fame as the leading architects, furnishers and decorators of the finest mansions in the kingdom. They were in need of an artist who would carry out the particular Adam motif in the ornamental hardware and wall brackets which formed a necessary part of the decoration. In Boulton they found a kindred spirit who was ready to work with them. This will explain many of the pieces executed by Boulton which show a definite Adam influence.

Although Matthew Boulton is primarily identified with the Sheffield Plate trade, it is not to be thought that he did not produce many pieces in solid silver. Some of the finest examples of candelabra and other decorative pieces bear his hallmark. It was his association with the silver trade that resulted in the establishment of the assay offices in both Birmingham and Sheffield. In the manufacture of his solid silver wares he was faced with a serious obstacle which interfered with the rhythm of his production. The nearest office to which the silver could be taken for assaying was at Chester, which was seventy-two miles away. This involved long delays plus the risk of highway robbery which was quite prevalent at the time. This situation turned Boulton's mind to a study of the laws which governed the production of silver and for years he worked toward the establishment of an assay office at Birmingham. In 1772 he discussed this publicly and men in the city of Sheffield gave great heed to what the newspapers reported of Boulton's efforts. Naturally, they were quick to contact Boulton, for they too faced the same problems as the silversmiths of Birmingham. As befitted the character of the man, Boulton received them most graciously and requested an interchange of ideas plus a spirit of co-operation between the leaders of the two cities. Although great objections were raised by the London Goldsmiths Company against this new idea, assay offices were eventually established in both cities in 1773.

While we are primarily interested in Boulton's association with the Sheffield Plate trade, it would be remiss not to mention his greatest contribution to the world. This was the development of the steam engine and the furthering of the use of steam power, both of which eventually enabled Birmingham to become the greatest center in all Europe for the manufacture of heavy machinery. Boulton was responsible for the introduction of the rotating engine which has since been developed into a necessity in various types of manufacturing. Although his name is not known to the world at large, no greater credit could be given than that which James Watt bestowed on him by openly admitting that his production would have been a failure without the help of Boulton.

The amount of time which Boulton expended in his various business activities would have seemed more than enough to fill a lifetime for the ordinary man. However, Boulton busied himself with no end of local politics and in particular with the development of his city. Whether it was in a discussion of social reforms or perhaps a new bill requesting the reduction of taxes, the townspeople turned to Boulton for the leadership which was rarely if ever denied them.

In 1807 Boulton became seriously ill; and, after a long illness, he died on August 7, 1809 in his eighty-first year. The funeral was one of the greatest testimonials ever paid to a private citizen by a city. The procession included all those of business importance and social prominence as well as over six hundred workers from his various factories. Thousands and thousands of spectators lined the route of the hearse, for everyone sought to pay a simple tribute to the memory of a great man. Matthew Boulton was enormously successful from a financial standpoint in all his business dealings, and an examination of his will showed that he left an estate of over one hundred and fifty thousand pounds, which for those days was a handsome amount of money. Many engaged in the collection of old silver and Sheffield Plate will readily testify upon examination that the work of Matthew Boulton was outstanding to such a degree that it would not be an exaggeration to refer to him as the Rembrandt of his trade. No name is better known to the layman than his, for the words Fine Old Sheffield Plate and Matthew Boulton are almost synonymous.

Chapter Six

Articles Made in Sheffield Plate—I

❧

T HE FOLLOWING information does not pretend to be complete, for the reason that it would be well-nigh impossible to have knowledge of every effort of the platers' production. For the most part, pieces fall into selected categories, but then there are the hundreds of unusual bits which can be described only under the heading of miscellany. With reference to date we cannot be exact as to year and therefore use the term *circa,* "about." As we know, date letters were not used on Sheffield Plate, and so we place the time of production within a span of a few years. This is done primarily by judging the construction and design of a piece, for the progress in the trade is easily discernible on close study. Because many of the workers did not avail themselves of the privilege of registration, we again must assume identification from the particular style of each smith.

A mere handful of firms dominated the production of the trade, and it is not surprising, therefore, that we find constant repetition of the listing of these makers. The equipment which was a necessary factor in these plants was very costly and few firms were able to raise the required capital. We find that many of the lesser houses did nothing but reproduce pieces made by other houses, and these through the loan of dies. The spirit of co-operation which existed among rivals was noteworthy, and the implements of manufacture were generally available to those who could not afford their own. Purely from a business standpoint, the industry was very profitable for most firms who were solidly established. Local bankers were only too ready to provide additional capital to those who were outstanding, and to supply them with the sorely needed funds for the expansion of their wares. In addition, they were able to attract workmen from the London silver houses, since they could offer high wages with a guarantee of lower living costs in Sheffield.

It is interesting to note that statistics record that a silversmith with a particular talent would work for several factories during the course of a year. If he excelled as a chaser he might complete an order with one firm, and then carry on his work at a rival organization. In this way he earned considerably more money, and the entire trade had the benefit of his individual skill. Proof of this is found on those pieces which bear the initials of an identified silversmith, and yet carry makers' marks of several different firms.

The spirit of brotherhood among rival houses is further evidenced from the histories of the trade that record the loan and interchanging of parts of articles. In other words, if one company specialized in the production of bobeches or nozzles, they were only too willing to loan their dies, perhaps in exchange for others they did not possess. The primary purpose of this was to enlarge the general scope of manfacture, for the trade knew that if it prospered as a group, its individual members would reap the harvest.

In the ensuing pages are examples identified as the major works of the Sheffield platers, although it is not an uncommon occurrence to find identical ones manufactured in solid silver. This is readily understandable, for if a firm owned the dies, they found it expedient to produce the same article in both silver and plate, as an impetus to additional business. However, an attempt has been made to associate the workings in plate as a group, in order that the reader may not become too confused.

BOXES

The instant popularity of Sheffield Plate boxes was rather fantastic. Although one of the first items produced by the new process, they were accorded immediate acceptance that guaranteed their makers full-scale production. Boxes have always held a peculiar fascination, for in a way they are personal, private and often precious to the owner beyond their intrinsic value. There have probably been more collectors of boxes throughout the history of art than of any other object, and the types have included a wide range from tobacco holders to pill boxes.

The earliest specimens were molded with pull-off covers, for neither Boulsover nor Hancock had developed his ability sufficiently to provide well-made hinges. Many display evidence of fine hand chasing, while others were struck from cut steel dies. So well established was the trade of box making that we find instances of apprentices being trained for nothing but the production of boxes. However, their popularity continued for only about fifteen years, and therefore we may definitely date the span of their manufacture from 1750 to 1765.

Early Sheffield boxes are readily recognized by their lack of tinning on the inside. In all probability this was a means of economy, for the early platers found it necessary to market a product that would compete favorably with the well-established silver trade. The majority of boxes were used to contain tobacco, snuff or money, although one sees smaller units used to hold patches and aromatic sponges. The Cutlers Company records the existence of a specially organized box trade.

Although box making had its start in the city of Sheffield, it was eventually taken over by the jewelers in Birmingham. Specimens from the former city are very, very rare, and there are not many collectors who have ever assembled more than an isolated few. Many of the boxes display a strong foreign influence in design. We particularly allude to the French craftsmen, who may have originally manufactured the boxes in copper and then sent them to England for plating. On the other hand, many were marked with English lettering, which would seem to indicate they were home products.

BUCKLES

Prominent among the efforts of the pioneer platers were shoe buckles. Examples in plate are known to have existed as early as 1660, although the method by which they were made is too obscure to justify any confident statement as to its nature. Buckles were in great demand by those attached to the court, for each costume required a separate set. In view of the readiness of those of the wealthier classes to indulge the slightest whims with regard to dress and appearance, the prosperity of the trade of buckle making is only too apparent.

In effect, the majority made during the early period were not examples of plating by fusion, for this process presented major difficulties in their production. In order to reduce the buckles to their required thickness, a great amount of hammering was involved. Inasmuch as the base metal was soft, few perfect specimens resulted. For this reason, the majority were made by the process of close plating. Buckles existed in gold as well as silver, although gold buckles were confined to those of extreme wealth. Other types encountered were made in iron, pinchbeck and gilded brass. For the most part, the designs keynoted simplicity with an applied decoration of steel ornamented by cutting. It is from these that the jewelry trade learned the art of making marcasite brooches and bracelets.

BUTTONS

The first articles made by the Sheffield Plate process were buttons, and considerable skill was shown in their construction. Although the majority were made from fused copper plate, many were struck from dies used for solid silver buttons made during the Queen Anne period, 1702 to 1714. The original process of button making is still employed today, for in this one field the process of electroplating has not been found to be practicable.

Manufacturers of buttons had within their grasp a lucrative industry, and firms have been traced as having been in the business since 1700. The majority of plated buttons were used in the outfitting of servants, and often bear the crest of the household in which the domestic was employed. Others were decorated with the initial of a family, which readily indicates that their use was not confined to those of Royal patronage.

Although the industry is not highly regarded today, it was formerly considered of great importance. Early in the eighteenth century, the Cutlers Company of Sheffield engaged in a long and costly defense of the trade, even though the organization was beyond its jurisdiction. The victory on behalf of the button makers was a great stimulus to the trade in Sheffield, and it is not surprising that Boulsover's first efforts found such a ready reception.

Buttons were made in a variety of materials including horn, brass and an amalgam known as alcomy. While Sheffield Plated buttons did not displace the others, they filled the wants of those intermediate classes who could not afford solid silver but whose taste for luxury was satisfied by an article that so closely resembled it.

Communion Services

The permanence of Sheffield Plate wares is best exemplified by its acceptance for use in the church. Although we find only one specialist in this field, his contributions were numerous, and examples of the work of Robert Gainsford may still be seen today. There is little doubt that these were made for parishes in small communities who could not afford sets in solid silver.

Gainsford was a Roman Catholic and he received his greatest support from those of his faith. Included in his catalogue of available pieces were altar candlesticks and cruets, ciboriums, communion cups, patens, pix boxes, and incense burners. Although this trade of church plate did not flourish throughout the industry in England, it was one of the leading productions of the French makers and there are many existing examples of French communion services.

Chapter Seven

Articles Made in Sheffield Plate—II

❧

Condiment Sets

THE important trade which was carried on between England and India was responsible for the introduction of condiments into Great Britain. Rare spices were a natural accessory to the inviting dishes which were offered in the homes to appease the appetite of the Englishman. While English food today is not generally of a highly seasoned nature, during the sixteenth and seventeenth centuries the presence of condiments even to an excessive state is noted. We can attribute this to the high cost of spices, for anything that was rare and expensive appealed to those who were on the constant search for luxuries. This led quite naturally to the production of salt cellars, pepper pots and mustard pots in addition to the graceful and lovely cruet stands which combined many condiments in one frame. We shall deal primarily with salt, as its history is fascinating and the containers throughout silversmithing and plate making are always evidenced in great numbers.

Salts

The never-ending popularity of salt cellars can be directly traced to the varied superstitions inherited from the sixteenth century. The presence of salt on one's table in those days accomplished a dual purpose. First, it was thought that salt was the means by which evil spirits would be banished from one's home; second, the salt served as a marker in procedure for seating. In olden days, salt was the line of demarcation between servant and master and one was placed at the table either above

45

or below the salt according to his designated rank. This was accomplished by the use of a very small portion of salt which was placed in a magnificent silver container ofttimes thirty inches in height. However, the compartment in which the actual condiment was placed was barely three inches in diameter. These articles are known as standing salts and number among the most expensive and rare products of the early silversmiths' trade. The reason for the small quantity of salt was its rarity and, consequently, excessive cost. Salt, in those days, was not widely used as a seasoning for food, for not until one hundred years later was it available in quantities which permitted all to partake of it. It is said that upon being seated at a table a host would place a pinch of it on his lips, thereby assuring his guests that the food to be served would be harmless.

Sheffield Plate salt cellars of the early period were invariably oval in shape, with a pierced design, and mounted on four small feet. Those of this texture required crystal linings, the majority of which were of a dark blue hue. They reflected a delicacy that seems incongruous with the more elaborate pieces that were produced at the same time. Yet, they proved beyond a doubt the versatility of the early plater, for he had a talent which was constantly appearing in the production of some new object. During the later years of the Sheffield Plate period, salt cellars lost most of their artistic appeal and suffered greatly from overembellishment.

Unfortunately, the acquisition of early examples is difficult, for while the frames are still available many of the original glass linings have been broken and replaced with reproductions. Even an inexperienced amateur collector will perceive at a glance the difference between a piece of original crystal, with its many imperfections, and a modern one. Salts were made in even numbers ranging from matching pairs to sets of as many as sixteen units. Those that were constructed of solid metal presented a problem, for the action of salt on silver is destructive. It was only by gilding heavily the insides of the salt dishes that this problem was overcome, for while salt displays corrosive qualities on silver, it has no such effect on gold. During the early nineteenth century we encounter magnificent specimens of shaped Waterford crystals which were placed in a wire-type frame. Here again we note the close association between these two trades, although it is safe to say that these later types were far better examples of glass making than silversmithing.

Peppers

No rarer example of Sheffield Plate will be found than the pepper pot, as evidenced by the isolated few known today. Many of the firms which specialized in both the production of silver and plate listed among their efforts specimens of peppers in solid silver only, for it was not thought to be expedient to create them in the base metal. The few that have come to light are among the poorest examples of the plater's work, being of a very spindly construction and not truly durable.

Mustard Pots

Mustard pots are rare, and this seems difficult to understand, for they carried the body of a salt cellar fitted with a hinged cover. It is true that certain ones are known to have matched sets of salts, and if you are fortunate enough to acquire a complete service you may well feel gratified. The action on silver of mustard also required the use of crystal linings or gold plating. This destructive quality will be noticed with nearly every condiment that is known.

Salt Spoons

The query as to the whereabouts of Sheffield Plated salt spoons can be answered with one simple statement. Very rarely does one ever find pieces of this nature executed in plate; because of the relatively small size and low metallic content, they could have been just as easily and inexpensively produced in solid silver.

Cruet Stands

The English were very fond of condiments, as we have said. Therefore, it is no wonder that one finds so many cruet stands produced in Sheffield Plate. However, the mystery that will always surround these articles is where the unlimited quantities of beautiful bottles were obtained. Actually, the Sheffield platers' contribution to the cruet stand was nothing but the frame with a handle which held a group of two to eight bottles. These might include holders for oil and vinegar, a container with a pierced top for pepper or salt and a mustard pot fitted with a spoon. Cruet stands, or soy stands as they are often called, are indeed rare to find with all of their original fittings, for over a period of years many of the bottles may have been broken and replaced. An interesting sidelight is the combination wherein one finds the entire body made in Sheffield Plate with the metal tops of the bottles executed in solid silver. Throughout the history of the industry, we shall often find instances such as this, for the amount of metal to be used was so small that it was just as reasonable to make it in real silver as in plate. Cruet stands were made in a great variety of styles and shapes and are most pleasing to look upon, in addition to being well adapted for use today on the buffet table or in the preparation of salad dressings.

DRINKING ARTICLES

Since time immemorial, the possession of a personal drinking container is noted, and throughout the history of the world we are constantly aware of specimens in many different substances in the fields of either pottery or metal. Among the best works of the early silversmiths, dating as far back as the fourteenth century, were amazing flagons, pitchers and goblets which were produced with unbelievable skill. Many were authentic reproductions of early masterpieces in crystal and porcelain. Unfortunately, those which were made of a breakable content have not survived and for that reason we feel indebted to the silversmiths who created the museum specimens which may be viewed today.

Beakers and Tankards

It is readily understandable that the love of drinking would have led to the production of mugs and tankards on a large scale. People of extreme wealth imbibed from containers in solid silver; the others owned base metal tankards which were left at the local tavern, and the preference seemed to be for those made of pewter rather than plated ware.

Examples in Sheffield Plate are rare, although those that are available today invariably show their original ownership by the names engraved on them. While there was no set uniformity as to the size of tankards, the majority were made according to "Winchester Measure." This was the system of sizes prior to the institution of legalized weights and measures. Larger pieces were stamped with initials "I M" to denote "Imperial Measure." Interesting examples were made with a slit at the base of the handle. This was used as a whistle in order to summon the barkeeper when one's tankard needed refilling. There are also types which are referred to as peg tankards. These contained small pegs soldered to the inside which served as a measuring device, for often one was charged for his drink according to the number of pegs which were covered.

Among those platers who specialized in the production of tankards and beakers were Thomas Law, Nathaniel and Josephus Smith and John Love.

Punch Bowls and Wine Cisterns

The reigning popularity of large social functions such as balls and receptions provided the incentive for the silversmiths of the Georgian period to produce massive punch bowls and wine cisterns. Although examples in solid silver are available, there seems to be a dearth of their counterparts in Sheffield Plate. There is little doubt that the majority of the platers must have felt that these were beyond their ability and required far too much time to produce. Undoubtedly, there would have been dubious reception among the middle classes for goods of this type, for they were not the ones who entertained on a lavish scale. However, rare isolated pieces have come to light and most probably these were the work of those firms who engaged in the manufacture of both silver and plate. Among the most desirable of punch bowls was the Monteith. This was the name applied to a particular type of bowl with a removable serrated rim; and the story is told that it owes its name to the Earl of Monteith, who was known as one of England's most fashionably dressed men and introduced a long frock coat with a notched edge. It is said that this unusual design inspired a contemporary silversmith to fashion a bowl of similar pattern. Actually the Monteith was a most practical bowl, for the notches were made in such a way that they held the stems of glasses and permitted them to be chilled by the ice prior to the service of the punch. The size of these bowls varied from extra large capacities to those which would normally serve eighteen to twenty people. The majority display a fluted design which is most pleasing and of high-quality workmanship.

The author has never seen a Sheffield Plated wine cistern of English manufacture, although undoubtedly they existed. The cistern differed from a bowl both in shape and size and was generally of gigantic proportion and oval, mounted on a solid foot. To those who have never seen one it is hard to conceive of their size, for many measure four feet in length with a content of many gallons. There is today no sale whatsoever for pieces such as these; even if they were adapted to present-day use as holders for ferns, they would dwarf any normal-size room.

Coasters and Wine Wagons

Although coasters were among the most varied products of the Sheffield Plate era they hold little interest for collectors. The vast number of these now available has lessened their relative value yet many are among the best efforts of their makers.

The service of wine was part of every meal and inasmuch as the vintage was decanted into attractive crystal bottles, the coaster served a necessary purpose. Its primary use was to prevent the bottom of the decanter from leaving a ring on the table. For this reason, it was inevitable that an attractive coaster would be introduced, as the wine was left on the table during the entire service of a meal. This custom permitted guests to refill their glasses at will.

The earliest known specimens in Sheffield Plate appeared about 1775 and showed a pierced design which was both attractive and popular. For about twenty-five years, extreme simplicity was the keynote of their construction and little change is noted until about the year 1815. At this time the makers of Sheffield Plate were highly skilled in the delicate arts of chasing and embossing, and many coasters were embellished with motifs of grapes and leaves directly allied to the vintage drink.

The natural outcome of the coaster was the wine wagon, which was really a combination of two or three coasters soldered together and mounted on movable wheels. This permitted the wine to be rolled about the table with great ease so that the guests might partake of their drink without waiting to be served individually. The origin of the wagon has been traced to the inventive genuis of Sir E. Thomson of Birmingham who first introduced it at the suggestion of His Majesty King George III. Wine wagons are quite desirable. Apart from their original use, they are ideal containers for candies and sweetmeats and are well suited for the holding of small flower pots.

Decanter Stands

One of the most pleasing combinations to be found in Sheffield Plate is the decanter stand. It incorporates the beauty of fine crystal with the simple structure of a well-proportioned holder for bottles. It is a testimonial to the Sheffield plater's art that he realized that finely cut crystal decanters would be set off most advantageously when placed in frames of extreme simplicity. Decanter stands were invariably of three or four sections, each of which was fitted with a bottle around whose neck was hung an attractive descriptive label. The trend toward practicability among the products of the Sheffield platers is evidenced in these. Each was equipped with an extra ring into which the stopper of the bottle could be placed as the wine was being poured. Many were fitted with brightly tinted bottles, originals of which are eagerly sought by buyers today. Although the general practice is to serve liquid refreshment in the container in which it is purchased, those who are fortunate enough to possess decanter stands are only too eager to decant their wines and liquors. There is something rather pleasing to the eye in a stand fitted with three or four filled decanters, each containing a differently colored liquid.

Here again we find a definite association between the industries of Sheffield Plating and glass making, for the resulting products could only have been produced by close unity between the masters of each trade.

Crystal decanters being unfortunately of a breakable nature were often destroyed during the years of their usage. Therefore, the reader is advised that close inspection be made, to be assured that the stoppers of the bottles are original and that all the decanters are matched. A rather popular recent innovation is the use of decanter stands bereft of their bottles as holders for plants.

Pitchers and Jugs

The word pitcher brings to mind in our present-day life a rather large graceful container for ice water. However, the examples produced in Sheffield Plate were made for a far different purpose. Pitchers were used primarily for the service of hot chocolate or wine; and for that reason were made with rather narrow necks which do not lend themselves to modern service where ice cubes are a necessity. The only examples which are practical for this use are the oversized jugs and basins which were used in hotels for washing. However, being of such large capacity they are practically impossible to handle when filled with water.

Jugs were produced as early as 1765 and at no time were they made in great quantities. Examples which closely followed the shapes of the George II beer jugs are practically unknown although they would be the only ones that would properly lend themselves for use today.

Wine Coolers

Every aspirant to the title of collector in Sheffield Plate invariably aspires to the ownership of a pair of wine coolers. These are purchased for their magnificence, and undoubtedly represent the apex of the platers' art. They are certainly not among the early efforts, for only a few are known prior to 1800, while the majority are of the late George III and early George IV periods. Their popularity was instantaneous and before long they replaced candelabra as the ornaments on one's sideboard. The majority were of highly decorative design with a definite trend toward the vintage pattern. However, those who are truly collectors look for the simple type, as they are rarer and probably blend into our present homes more decoratively. Nearly all wine coolers followed a very definite construction, containing a removable holder for the wine bottle around which the ice was placed. Those that were circular in shape are most plentiful and there is no doubt that they were the easiest type for the platers to produce. However, occasionally one encounters a square set, demonstrating the constant desire of the platers to venture far afield from the commonplace.

Here again we note that a handful of manufacturers specialized in the production of a particular type of article. A careful inspection of wine coolers will immediately prove how perfectly the platers had overcome every hardship of their craft, for the borders were intricately molded and applied with a skill not equalled in other articles. Many buyers today have found that coolers are excellent as containers for flowers or as mantel decorations, and this has led to their rise in value and the creation of a firm market for them. Occasionally one encounters suites of four or six matching units which will give an idea of the scale in which people entertained in former times.

Although we have mentioned numerous styles and designs in which wine coolers were executed, special mention must be made of the type which was reproduced from the incomparable vase at Warwick Castle. The history of the original piece is of extreme interest. It was made in white marble and attributed to the craftsmanship of the Grecian sculptor Lysippus (circa 325 B.C.) during the reign of Alexander the Great. The original is of huge proportions and measures five feet seven inches in height with a diameter of eight feet. It was discovered in 1770 at the bottom of Lake Pantanello, near Tivoli. It was brought to England in 1774 and sold to the Earl of Warwick in whose home it has since remained. The original vase may be numbered among the world's greatest art treasures. It was only through the courtesy of the Earl of Warwick that the vase was allowed to be copied in silver and later in Sheffield Plate. However, the reproductions which were made were on a far smaller scale, although they adhered in their relative proportions to the original size.

Wine Labels

Normally, in the history of an industry, it would be remiss to discuss specifically articles as unimportant as the small tags of identification which were placed around the necks of decanters. However, such an unbelievable amount of effort was expended in their manufacture that they demand more than just passing mention. A close inspection of liquor labels of the Georgian era, both in silver and plate, makes them the perfect target for the collector with limited means. The styles were so varied and of such exquisite design that one might well assemble two to three hundred different types with nary a duplication. Unfortunately, many of the names describing the vintages are not in popular demand today, and the average collector desires only the possession of labels with the names of rye, scotch and bourbon. However, inasmuch as these liquors were practically unknown at that time, one must be willing to make the sacrifice and be satisfied with the creations that indicate the drinks then popular.

Wine Funnels and Tasters

Only passing reference need be made to such isolated examples of Sheffield Plate as wine funnels, strainers and tasters. Although specimens have been unearthed, proving beyond a doubt that these were numbered among the products of the platers, only a few were made. It was, doubtless, their comparatively low cost in solid silver that discouraged the makers of Sheffield Plate from producing these pieces in any quantity. However, if you are fortunate enough to own an example you should treasure it, for it is rare.

FLATWARE

A review of the history of the efforts of the Sheffield platers seems like an endless success story until one is confronted by the category which includes knives, forks, and spoons. It may definitely be stated that attempts in this direction met with dismal failure and at no time could the industry be proud of the eating utensils it created. Perhaps it was the well-established methods then in use by the cutlers that discouraged workers from trying to improve on their original efforts. At any rate, the earliest examples that we have inherited have completely shed the silver plating with which they were originally covered and have been reduced to a bare state. This group includes flimsy teaspoons and sugar tongs which were beaten out from drawn wire with flat chasing on the shanks. On these one will encounter rather unusual marks not generally found on other specimens of Sheffield Plate. These include "Best Plate," "Plated" and "Silver Solder."

The hardships of manufacture discouraged any further attempts in this field although several pieces such as soup ladles, caddy spoons, and fish slicers are occasionally encountered. It was not until the introduction of electroplating that the manufacturers of flatware were able to cope successfully with the problems that had formerly restrained them, for the new process completely revolutionized their production. Strangely, those engaged in electroplating were so proficient in the production of knives, forks and spoons, that within a short time the city of Sheffield became the world center for the industry.

A variance is noted in a product called Argentine which was a newly discovered base metal introduced about 1833. The firm of William Hutton and Sons is credited with being the first to use this. Although never extensively used in England, Argentine is frequently encountered in the study of foreign plate.

INKSTANDS

The first attempts at the manufacture of inkstands by the platers produced flimsy specimens, few of which have weathered the ravages of hard wear. For the most part they were of a pierced decoration and were reproduced exactly from previously made silver ones. It was not until 1800 that any individuality was shown in their construction, and at that time we note styles which had never been formerly known. As a general rule, the inkstand followed a definite pattern of style, being mounted on an under tray containing two wells and a taper box. Some of the center wafer boxes were surmounted by a small taperstick which served as the flame to melt the wax used to seal letters. At the outset, inkstands were small in size and these are the ones in constant demand. Other larger styles followed, including the massive Ambassador types fitted with a removable drawer. In shape, most were oblong, although the most pleasing types were the boat-shape examples. Other rare specimens include the small globular ones which were enclosed between circular folding sides, mounted on a foot.

Relative to the purchase of inkstands, it is of the utmost importance to scrutinize the wells, for the originals of crystal may have been broken and replaced.

LIGHTING APPLIANCES

Candlesticks

Holders for candles are mentioned as early as 1500 B.C. and even at that early date were wrought with considerable attention to beauty and design. Although candles are no longer necessities, we still retain a love for the soft glow and warmth that emanate from their flickering flames. Somehow or other a meal eaten by candlelight seems to have a warm and gentle touch. No doubt the popularity of candlelight will continue indefinitely, for above all its soft glow provides a flattering light that is dear to the hearts of women.

The earliest known example of a candlestick in Sheffield Plate is attributed to Josiah Hancock who produced a matching pair in the year 1755. This is truly amazing, for the construction of candlesticks involved many a difficult process and yet this worthwhile contribution to the industry was achieved during the first twelve years of its existence. Although the original efforts of Hancock were of a crude nature, they showed the path by which succeeding workers were enabled to produce the many hundreds of beautiful specimens in later years.

The first candlesticks were comprised of hoops soldered together and later swaged into their required shape. Unfortunately, this tended to give them an uneven and disproportionate appearance. Soft solder was generally used for connecting the various parts, with an extraordinary thickness of plating then applied. The first important improvement is noted in 1765, at which time a method was devised which permitted the candlestick to be made entirely from cast dies. The designs were primarily copied from the Ionic Column of Grecian times with fluted pillars and scroll capitals. Not until 1800 were interesting decorative borders achieved with any degree of success. The reason was the use of solid silver mounts whereas the earlier ones had been made with lead borders. Unfortunately, the use of lead was most impractical; after a few years of hard usage pitmarks and dents were easily discernible.

A major problem which confronted the manufacturers of candlesticks was that of stability, for it was necessary to have the base of sufficient weight in order to prevent the candlestick from toppling over. This problem was solved by the use of rosin with which the candlesticks were filled. Undoubtedly, this method was introduced through the medium of the many cutlers who were now engaged in the new industry, for by a similar process the handles of knives had previously been strengthened. Unfortunately, the filling of the bases with rosin did not give sufficient support to the column, for the rosin had nothing to which it could adhere. This brought about the introduction of an iron rod which ran throughout the entire candlestick, beginning at the base and terminating at the point where the bottom of the bobeche was fitted. Although this method achieved complete success in England, it presented a rather unusual problem to those manufacturers of candlesticks who exported their wares to foreign lands. Inasmuch as the climate in many of these countries was considerably warmer than that in England, it was found that the rosin would melt and leak out from the base. This problem was overcome by the substitution of plaster of Paris for the rosin.

A popular version of the candlestick was the telescopic type which permitted the light at the table to be raised or lowered at will. Although many ingenious methods were suggested and tried in the construction of these the most efficient of all devices was the one built on the Archimedean principle wherein the candle was affixed to a small spike at the base of the capital. We are especially indebted to the firms of Roberts, Cadman and Company and Ekhardt and Morton for perfecting this method.

In no field of endeavor did the vivid imagination of the silversmith run as wild as in the production of candlesticks. Specimens in Sheffield Plate were produced in a multitudinous array which included shaped bases varying from square, round and oblong to oval. The heights varied from three and one-half inches to those which reached the massive proportions of twenty-four inches. The latter were used either in the service of the church or to grace the dining table at baronial halls. Although many of the styles produced were copied indirectly from the architecture of the stone pillars used at the time of the Greeks and Romans, rarely were examples executed which might be termed authentic reproductions. For some reason each plater felt that it was necessary to add his own particular style of decoration in order to achieve a personalized product.

Among the many firms engaged in the production of candlesticks we find one that excelled not only for the high quality of its workmanship but also for the unbelievable number of specimens which it fostered. The firm of Winter, Parsons and Hall was known as the greatest candlestick maker in the city of Sheffield and undoubtedly many of the pieces it produced were supplied for the trade.

Although the average home of today requires the use of only two candlesticks, collectors are constantly seeking complete sets of four to eight matching pieces. When purchasing candlesticks, it is important to buy only those in which the bobeches are originals, for throughout the years many have been replaced. It is safe to assume that if a candlestick was made with a round base and gadroon border, the original bobeches would be of similar shape and decoration.

Candelabra

Candelabra were the natural outcome of candlesticks, and consisted of original bases upon which were mounted a pair of graceful arms. The primary purpose of the candelabra was to give additional light, although their decorative quality was important. In effect a candelabrum resembled a tree with arms spread out as from the bole of the trunk. Many of the types reflected designs which might have been copied from the forest. Actually, candelabra are among the most pleasing of all the articles produced in Sheffield Plate.

In this particular trade, we find the great Matthew Boulton the outstanding specialist, and specimens bearing his stamp are original for their combination of graceful line and proper proportion. Even a layman after a careful surveillance would identify them as the products of a great master. The majority of candelabra made during the Sheffield Plate period were rather large in stature, for the rooms for which they were fashioned combined both high ceilings and great length. So great was the expanse of many of the dining tables found in the homes of royalty, that it is not uncommon to find matching sets of candlesticks and candelabra consisting of from ten to twelve units used en suite.

The styles of candelabra varied greatly in decoration, although the majority followed a definite pattern of construction. The most usual example is that which consisted of two branches which held three candles, with the center one as a rule being below or above the sides. In addition, the center light was invariably fitted with a removable flame which permitted the candelabra to be used as a holder for two lights only, and yet have the appearance of a finished article. Another practical variation provided for the removal of the branches so that when the dining table was set for just a few people the base could be used as a single candlestick. The extreme, large size of original specimens has forced many people to purchase good reproductions that have been made on a smaller scale, for many of the homes of today with small rooms and dining alcoves do not provide sufficient space for the use of large pieces.

It is indeed rare to find small examples, and here again it is timely to say that those that are undersized are not necessarily better in style but rather more desirable, for they lend themselves to our present-day mode of living in a more adaptable manner.

Certain other variations of candelabra were made which permitted the silversmiths to give vent to their own particular creative ideas. Among the styles which met with great approval was the popular combination of a candelabrum with an epergne. Many pieces so designed had removable crystal dishes which permitted the insertion of small nozzles to hold candles. These would surround the center crystal bowl and give a most pleasing effect with the combination of fruit or flowers ringed by candlelight. Then there is the type so constructed that one can remove the arms from one candelabrum and place it atop the arms of the other, resulting in an unusual five-light structure. Most collectors prefer the acquisition of candelabra over the single-light candlesticks since they definitely combine far more beauty and grace. In addition, they lend a note of decoration not normally found in the use of candlesticks. To impress upon the reader the wide variations of both size and style, it is necessary only to mention that there are examples today of candelabra with as many as ten lights and reaching a height of nearly four feet.

In the purchase of candelabra, the author recommends close scrutiny of all parts. Frequently, one encounters specimens with branches not matching the base or else where the bobeches have been lost and replaced by others of a later date. It is well to bear in mind that the originals were made as matching units and examples should be purchased only in their proper condition. In other words, if the base is round, the shape of the capital and bobeches of the arms should be of matching design.

Chambersticks

There is no doubt that necessity was the mother of invention with regard to many of the implements which were devised by the silversmiths of the eighteenth century. Living in an age where candlelight was the sole source of illumination, it was only natural that their thoughts would have turned to attractive holders made in precious metal to accommodate the indispensable tapers. The most important in this group is the chamberstick, which as its name implies was used primarily for purposes of lighting in the bedroom. It was quite a common custom for a home of wealth to own a set of chambersticks which were available to each member of the family upon his nightly trip to his place of retirement. It is for this reason that it is not uncommon to find these made in matching sets of as many as sixteen, for, as we know, many of the early households were large and contained many bedrooms.

The general shape of chambersticks was circular or oblong, although oval types are occasionally encountered. As a rule a chamberstick was fitted with a scissors type of snuffer with which one could extinguish the candle when ready for bed. Unfortunately, many of the examples do not have their original snuffers. The earliest specimens in plate date from about 1770, although they were not produced in any great quantities until after 1810. The platers did little but copy from earlier examples made in solid silver. Another type which was popular was the chamberstick which was fitted with a conical-shaped extinguisher. Inasmuch as this could be produced for considerably less than that with the scissors type of snuffer it was far more popular. The chamberstick is used today as a decorative accessory on a desk or as a cigarette holder at the dining table.

Candle Snuffers

The candle snuffer was an article which greatly resembled a scissors and was generally made with an under tray to match. Although we know that these snuffers were at one time a necessity in the home, it is strange that so much effort should have been expended in their production by the Sheffield Platers. Yet, think of the present-day cigarette lighters and their infinite variations. Literally hundreds of inventions and patents for the manufacture of snuffers were introduced between the years 1750 and 1850. Probably the reason for their great popularity was the fact that the ordinary candle smoldered incessantly unless frequently snuffed. Indeed, the chore of lighting was then a laborious one and one may say that the silversmiths contributed more to relieving this problem than any other artisans. Snuffers and trays represent the perfect endeavor for the amateur collector, for they combine much of the best of the Sheffield platers' ability and yet are obtainable at low cost.

Tapersticks

A rather curious adaptation of the candlestick was the taper, which was but a miniature of the generally accepted lighting device. It was from three to four inches in height and its purpose was to hold a slender taper which was used for melting wax in order to seal letters. These tapers were frequently placed in the center of an inkstand where they formed an integral part of the writing apparatus. They are rare and constantly sought after for their decorative appeal.

Chapter Eight

Articles Made in Sheffield Plate—III

❧

SALVERS AND TRAYS

ALTHOUGH throughout the industry we often identify Sheffield wares as being but reproductions of earlier specimens in silver, the study of trays and salvers will refute this beyond doubt. In the manufacture of these wares, the platers raised the quality of their product to heights which had never before been reached, and introduced original creations that were beyond the dreams of contemporary silversmiths. It is with renewed respect for this short-lived industry that we gaze on the masterpieces that have survived.

A small circular waiter was listed as early as 1760 among the efforts of Josiah Hancock, and although of crude nature it provided the model from which thousands were to be made in the next seventy years. It may seem strange that so many were marketed, but Sheffield Plated trays were a necessity in the home and could be produced for relatively low cost. More than the usual care was expended in the manufacture of these, for trays were subjected to hard wear in their daily use.

The casual student of silver would normally assume that the earliest pieces would have been severely plain, with the thought in mind that those void of decoration would have entailed less labor. This was true except with the production of trays, for the large surfaces unfortunately brought into prominence imperfections which only decoration could conceal. It is conceivable that at a date as early as this in the industry the workers had not surmounted difficulties such as these. Therefore between the years 1760 and 1775, the majority of trays displayed chased centers with a noticeable lack of borders. The question of decorative relief on the edges was not answered until nearly thirty years afterwards when the platers at last learned the use of applied silver rims. This may be said to hold true of the application of feet. A further impetus to the manufacture of trays was noted in the introduction of the silver shield, for no article lent itself more admirably to the display of a coat of arms.

While the first fifty years of Sheffield Plating are not notable for the manufacture of waiters and trays, those that followed were truly remarkable for the heights of excellence attained. Between 1800 and the termination of the process, more trays were produced than any other article. An inspection of this array causes one to marvel at the scope and magnificence of the work. Trays of every imaginable shape, size and style were made, ranging from attractive six-inch card carriers to huge thirty-six-inch waiters for complete tea services. Until about 1815, the designs were rather fine, but shortly afterwards the demand for objects of highly chased design caused a considerable amount of overembellishment. While the later types were masterpieces of production they were sadly lacking in beauty and certainly do not fit appropriately in homes of today. Collectors are seeking the simpler types with well-molded gadroon borders and silver shields, for these are representative of the best.

In the field of foreign plate, trays seemed to have held the greatest attraction for the makers—the majority of Continental examples are listed in this category.

STAFFORDSHIRE WARE

The combination of plate with various articles in the field of ceramics is primarily identified with T. Law and Company. Although they specialized in the use of Staffordshire ware, pieces of theirs are known with bodies formed from coconuts, horn and ivory. We particularly stress the beautiful jugs with decoration in high relief. The jasper or stoneware was generally of a tinted color combining brown and white, or the blue and white attributed to Wedgwood. It is logical to assume that these found a ready market, for both the industry of plating and the potting of Staffordshire reached the heights of excellence at approximately the same time.

These pieces are not especially noteworthy as contributions of the plater, for the mounts were invariably done in extreme simplicity. It is to the beautiful pottery that we pay special heed, for the designs copied from the immortal Flaxman are indeed splendid. Through the years, few of these have remained in a decent state of preservation, and examples in prime order are precious.

SUPPER SERVICES

Beware of the antique supper dish, for more reproductions of these are offered as genuine than any other article of high value. Because of the greater numbers of entree dishes and soup tureens available, one can with little effort combine a matching set and place them in a new base. These made-up services should not be sold as being completely original, yet they are offered daily. A completely old supper dish is very rare and, when available, commands a price that few are willing to pay. Yet, buyers in their anxiety to own pieces of Sheffield Plate rarely inspect them to authenticate age. Today in America, the supper service has found a ready market among those who entertain at large buffet suppers or cocktail parties.

Supper dishes were originally placed in the center of a large table to permit the guests to partake of the various delicacies without being served individually. This was accomplished in simple manner, as the dishes were mounted on bases which allowed them to revolve when turned. It is from this idea of saving on service that the name "Lazy Susan" came.

TABLEWARE

Argyles

The term "argyle" refers to a container with a hot-water jacket which was used for the service of gravy or sauce. It differed from the accepted type of tureen or sauce boat in that it was made with a double lining into which hot water or burning embers were placed. The exact derivation of the name has never been properly traced, although the generally accepted story is that a piece of this nature was made by a silversmith, by special order of the Duke of Argyle, whence it took its name. Argyles were originally introduced in solid silver during the latter part of the reign of George II, and most of the examples in Sheffield Plate were reproductions of the earlier types. These were not known prior to 1785, but after their introduction enjoyed great popularity as evidenced by the number of different styles produced. The most common shape was that which looked like a stunted coffee pot, although specimens varied from the appearance of a tea pot to that of a sauce tureen. From the standpoint of practicability argyles were desirable, for in those days the serving pantry was a good distance from the dining table and the argyle served to keep the sauces reasonably well heated. Although the manufacture of argyles was not an intricate process, the repairing of the jacket, in case of damage, was most difficult.

Baskets

Bread baskets were produced in greater quantities than nearly any other article in Sheffield Plate, for the need of some kind of bread basket was almost universal. Even in the poorer groups an attractive wooden or base metal container was always noted on a dining table. Baskets were made in various shapes, generally with a swing handle, which permitted each person at the table to pass the dish with ease.

Sheffield Plated examples were introduced about 1770 and became instantly popular with those who could ill afford the costly solid silver specimens. Probably no other article of the early period exhibited such beautiful workmanship of the Sheffield makers as these bread baskets, most of which incorporated a combination of fine hand piercing with a delicate type of chasing or engraving. The early types are those most desired by collectors, for the later ones did not reflect the graceful proportions and fine workmanship. The first baskets produced were oval or oblong in shape, wherein they followed the contemporary examples in solid silver. Hundreds of different types of bread and cake baskets were made during the Sheffield Plate era. About the year 1800, silver edges of ornamental design were introduced; the earliest specimens had simple borders with only a flange of delicate piercing.

Baskets have now lost much of their functional appeal except as containers for fruit or flowers; in present-day service, bread is no longer placed centrally on the table.

Cheese Dishes

Many articles made during the Sheffield Plate period are in use in the home of today yet only a scattered few are employed in their original capacity. Refuting this statement, however, is the cheese dish which is now used for the service of toasted hors d'oeuvres much in the same manner as in the early nineteenth century. The cheese or bacon container resembled a flat oblong dish fitted with a cover. It invariably housed at its base a compartment for hot water so that the savories that were placed in it did not lose flavor by chilling. In addition there was usually a wooden or ivory handle. At the point where the handle met the dish there was an opening through which hot water was poured. There is no doubt that its origin may be traced to the argyle which as we know contained a jacket for the heating of food or liquid. The savories that were served in olden days were made of thin slices of cheese which were placed on corresponding squares of bread. They were heated in an oven and then served with the pre-dinner drink. In similar manner, the dish is used today along with the service of cocktails. Many of the early specimens were fitted with six individual compartment dishes so that by the use of a spatula the entire unit could be transferred from the stove into the cheese dish.

The popularity of cheese dishes is fully evidenced by the great variety of shapes and styles made. The exquisite workmanship that was exerted in their manufacture by the early platers endears them to every lover of silver. The present-day silent butler is patterned on the Sheffield cheese dish, minus the hot water compartment.

Dinner Plates and Meat Dishes

Few dinner plates have survived from the Sheffield Plate era and even those that are available today hold little appeal. Although plates in solid silver were made in great numbers for the homes of the rich, the manufacturers in plate paid little attention to their production. There was no market for them. None but the rich cared for the luxury of silver plates. As for today, plates in precious metal for the service of meat and desserts have been superseded by wares of pottery or porcelain.

However, there are some examples of plates mounted on circular hot water containers. It is sometimes thought that these were used for invalids, but I doubt that. They are quite inefficient and the water tends to spill over the sides.

Although dinner services in Sheffield Plate are desirable when complete, they are very rare. An entire dinner service would have embraced both meat and soup plates as well as tureens, platters and entree dishes. Our homes today are unable to house services such as these and for this reason, when and if they are offered for sale, they are almost invariably dismantled into small units.

With regard to plates, the author wishes to sound a note of caution. Beware of sets that are nothing but reproductions with turned-over borders that simulate the originals. Perhaps the worst effrontery of all is the offering of antique butter plates which are often available to match the larger pieces. Butter plates were absolutely unknown in the Sheffield Plate era and are distinctly a modern development.

Dish Covers

The dish cover has fallen into disuse. In these days of simplified service it is not only oversized but impractical. It seems a shame, for the platers devoted the best of their talent to the production of these handsome objects which at the time of their original manufacture were in daily use in English homes. The primary purpose of the dish cover was to fit over a metal or china platter in order to keep the food hot while it reposed on the sideboard. One often finds matched sets of varied sizes in groups as large as twelve to fifteen pieces. At the present time there is little demand for them, and one may purchase fine originals for just a few dollars.

An interesting use of the dish cover has appeared during the past ten years. The piece is cut directly in half while the handle is still attached. By inverting these semi-covers and supplying backs for them, they may be used as attractive wall containers for flowers or plants. This innovation has met with considerable popularity and has caused a renewed search for interesting examples in old plate.

The type most in demand is that on which the coat of arms is set in a silver shield. It is necessary, then, to cut this part out and reverse it, or else the arms will be displayed upside down when the cover is used on the wall.

In size, covers ranged from ten to twenty-four inches in length and are today frequently used in hotels and fashionable restaurants.

Dish Rings

A study of the production of silver in Ireland discloses the fact that dish rings were among the most popular silver articles in Erin. Their appearance in Sheffield Plate is strange, for at no time were they especially popular in England. Therefore, one can only draw the inference that these rings were made exclusively for the Irish market. The dish rings made in Sheffield Plate differed from those made in Irish silver, for the latter ones usually portrayed rural subjects such as farm scenes, while the Sheffield Plated ones bore flat chased scroll and festoon ornamentation. They even differed in shape; all the Irish specimens were circular while those in plate were generally oval. That is why the Irish ones are always referred to as hash rings while plated ones are called dish rims. There has been much comment on the subject of their original use, and they are often referred to as potato rings with the intimation that a bowl of potatoes was placed on top the ring in order to preserve the surface of the table. However, many authorities on the subject claim that their use was for the purpose of holding a fine porcelain bowl in order to give it greater prominence and height. The generally accepted conclusion would indicate that these rings were used for both purposes, as not only were they interesting decorative adjuncts to a table but were most practical in the service of hot foods.

Entree Dishes and Warmers—Chafing Dishes

The entree dish or vegetable dish represented one article which for several reasons enjoyed far more popularity in plate than in silver. Its extreme weight in solid silver made it costly and impractical to use for convenient serving. Furthermore, when hot foods are placed in it, a silver container quickly absorbs heat and is extremely difficult to handle. Here we see for the first time the preference for plate over silver for practical reasons rather than purposes of economy.

Entree dishes enjoyed a long span of production that started about 1780, and even at the present time they are among the leading articles made by factories. They are durable and not excessively expensive.

The early specimens were made with stationary handles on both sides of the cover. However, shortly after the introduction of the removable lock handle this practice was discontinued. Those with the lock handles permitted the covers to be used as companion dishes to the bases and were usually fitted with an inner matched border.

Throughout the history of the service of food in England, we find that silverware was manufactured with more than an eye to utility. In the days when kitchens were far removed from dining rooms the food often arrived at the table cold and hardly palatable. This was overcome by the introduction of warmers into which entree dishes were fitted prior to being used in service. These warmers were either filled with hot water or else equipped with a compartment to hold small live charcoal. In our scheme of living today, we find little need for these warmers and yet they have been turned to good advantage, notably as attractive containers for plants.

Many variations of what are termed entree dishes were introduced during the Sheffield Plate era. Among these were hash, chafing and double dishes. This last category included large circular servers which were modeled along the principles of the bacon or cheese dish. They were equipped with removable wooden handles which provided an opening through which hot water could be poured to fill the jacket that encompassed the dish. The immensity of the households for which these articles were made may be judged by the sets of all types of entree dishes, many of which were made in four to eight matching units.

The chafing dish (literally, warming dish) is used nowadays chiefly for cooking at the table. But there is little doubt that the construction of the average large household in England in the eighteenth and nineteenth centuries was responsible for its introduction. In effect it was little more than an entree dish which was placed on a stand equipped with a heating device such as a small alcohol lamp with a wick. The heat of the lamp kept the food at a proper temperature during its long trek from the kitchen to the dining table. However, chafing dishes and heating stands did not come into general use until early in the Victorian era. The reason for their popularity then was because of the large hunt breakfasts which much of English nobility attended. At that time the dishes were placed on the sideboard for the riders who returned from the hunt. The popularity of this custom caused great production of dishes equipped with burners, and in this category we may mention heating stands. The heating stand was constructed of a simple frame at the base of which was placed from one to three alcohol lamps. The top of the stand consisted of a removable aluminum plate which acted as a safeguard against any damage that might be caused by the heat to the dishes that were placed upon it. During the last few years these heating stands have become extremely popular at large cocktail parties where they are found to be convenient in the service of hot hors d'oeuvres.

Epergnes and Plateaux

The epergne is frequently regarded as the article in which the plater reached the zenith of his ability. In these wondrous table centers he achieved a quality of workmanship that has rarely been surpassed. No doubt it was the freedom of artistic endeavor which prompted this, for here he had no set or specified object to reproduce. Epergnes were primarily articles of decoration and required little attention to practicability. It is to the Sheffield platers that we are indebted for the exquisite combination of plate and crystal. Although the earliest specimens were extremely simple in design and generally of wire structure, the later endeavors blossomed into veritable masterpieces of grandeur. The crystals were generally of a finely cut Waterford pattern while the holders were richly embossed with either decorations of foliage combined with acanthus leaves or ornate vintage motifs.

The immensity of the dining halls in those days caused many epergnes to be made of huge proportions. Unfortunately, these are not adaptable to our present style of living and it is for this reason that smaller examples fetch the highest prices when offered for sale.

Frequently, epergnes were made to match massive candelabra, entire groups being placed on sectional mirrored plateaux. The effect of the gleaming crystal in the shadow of the flickering light of the candelabra transferred an ordinary dining table into a spectacle of beauty. Another variation was the epergne which, set on a revolving base, held fruit in the center dish with a selection of sweetmeats in the side crystals. Although we eagerly seek fine specimens such as these, it is rare to encounter epergnes that are in their original state of manufacture. Through years of use the glass dishes may have been broken and, therefore, we caution the buyer to seek expert advice as to the authenticity of the fittings, for only those which are completely original merit the collector's efforts.

Sauce Boats, Tureens and Pipkins

In most cases sauce tureens were nothing but miniatures of soup tureens, although many were equipped with under plates to catch the dripping from the gravy. They were invariably sold in pairs and fetch high prices today, for they are admirable containers for candy. Tureens were extremely popular and are among the best endeavors of the platers, judged from the variety of styles that we have inherited.

The sauce boat was of entirely different shape and design although used primarily for the same purpose as the tureen. However, examples in Sheffield Plate are rare, few having been produced. This is probably due to their impracticability, for they lacked protective covers. They are known as early as 1760 and invariably follow the designs of earlier examples in solid silver.

Far more unusual than either of the above are sauce pans, or pipkins as these containers are often called. Their main use was in the heating of brandy, and they were equipped with wooden handles which served as protection against the flame that was applied to the under parts. Specimens in Sheffield Plate are rarely encountered, for they bespeak a luxury confined to those of extreme wealth.

Soup Tureens

While the soup tureen is normally associated with the old English dining table, it is the product of the inventive genius of a French silversmith. It is said that the name was derived from Marshal Turenne of France who while engaged in battle removed his helmet and used it as a container for soup. It is entirely within the bounds of possibility that a neophyte silversmith, who may have been among his men, was inspired with this sight and eventually created a container, giving it the marshal's name.

However, the English silversmiths went further afield with the production of these pieces in silver and plate than did their own French brothers. Practically no meal was considered complete unless it started with soup, and for that reason it was only natural that the reception for these containers would have been an immediate one. It was not unusual for tureens to be made in sets of four so that the many guests at a table would be served simultaneously, with the soup properly heated. Examples in Sheffield Plate are quite easy to obtain, for the platers were most prolific in this particular field.

While soup tureens are normally pieces of oversized proportions, there are many that lend themselves admirably to the modern dining room. As the name implies, a tureen was usually placed at the head of the table for the purpose of serving soup. Its present-day use is entirely different—a decorative centerpiece for the dining table. For those with refectory dining tables, there are oblong and oval styles available while for those who prefer the old-fashioned round table there are specimens of circular type. In addition, the tureen accomplishes another purpose. Being equipped with a removable cover, it may be used for flowers or fruit or else as a complete unit of decoration. The same would normally not apply to a bowl, for centerpieces which are void of covers require some sort of ornamentation.

Although the earliest soup tureen was produced in 1704 through the genius of Anthony Nelme, it was not until 1785 that the Sheffield platers made their contributions in this field to the industry. Unfortunately, we cannot point with particular pride to the specimens produced in plate, for at no time were they representative or symbolic of the magnificent creations made in solid silver by such master craftsmen as Paul Storr and Benjamin Smith.

TEA SERVICES

The function of the service of tea is performed with much dignity in England. For nearly four centuries the tea hour has been an integral part of each Englishman's day; and regardless of his station in life, a time for the imbibing of tea is allotted to everyone. Artisans in many different fields of endeavor have exerted their fullest efforts in the production of pieces used for the service of tea.

While we today visualize a tea service as a set of five or six matching units with a tray, it is important to understand that at the outset of the silver industry pieces were produced as single items. Not until 1790 do we note the appearance of matching tea pots, sugar bowls and creamers. During the next thirty years, coffee pots and tea kettles to match were included.

The introduction of tea to the English people was first noted in an advertisement that appeared in a London newspaper in 1658. However, it was not until six years later when the East India Company presented a pound of tea to His Majesty Charles II that it was formally introduced to the ladies and gentlemen of the Court. At first tea was used primarily for medicinal purposes, and certain types of home brews concocted from the tea leaves were thought to have great powers of healing. Although tea was unbelievably expensive at first, its instant popularity was the cause of its importation on a large scale; and by the year 1720, although still costly, it was available at a price which many families could afford. It is recorded that many people overindulged themselves to the extent of drinking as many as twenty to twenty-five cups per day.

Tea Pots

By the time the Sheffield Plate industry was in full production, tea had definitely been established as the English national drink and it is, therefore, with little surprise that we encounter the multitude of examples of tea pots in plate made between 1770 and 1830. These styles, shapes and sizes encompassed such a variety that one might well devote many chapters to the study of tea pots alone. The demand was so great that there was a ready market for the many types of tea pots which were devised by the silversmiths and platers. Actually, no home was considered complete without a proper tea pot either in solid silver, base metal or pottery.

The earliest examples did not incorporate the use of metal handles, for as yet the platers had not learned the art of insulation. Consequently, those examples made during the first stages of the industry had handles of either ebony, wood or ivory. In addition, there was a matching knob on the cover which permitted the lid to be raised for the refilling of the pot without causing the server to burn his or her fingers. Many of the early specimens were equipped with small matching under trays known as tea pot stands. Their primary purpose was to prevent the tables upon which the pots were placed from becoming scarred by the heat of the tea. However, the introduction of the ornamental leg or foot which overcame this problem caused these stands to be discarded, and it is indeed rare to find an example extant today with its original under tray.

Although for the most part pieces were individually produced, shortly after 1800 sets of four matching units were available. Unfortunately, because of a rather curious custom of willing individual pieces of one's tea service to various heirs, the component parts have long since been separated. It is only after diligent searching that it is sometimes possible to reassemble a service in its original state.

Coffee Pots and Biggins

The earliest known coffee pots were for the most part exact reproductions of ones that had been made at an earlier date in solid silver. It is a testimonial to the ability of the early platers that these were produced only fifteen years after the discovery of the Sheffield process. It is due, in great measure, to the fact that the earlier specimens were made with little thought to the cost of manufacture, that we have inherited many in truly excellent condition. For, at the time these coffee pots were first made, the business of plating had not become an industry, no general formula for the relationship between the content of silver and copper had been established, and many pieces had an extraordinary percentage of silver.

Many of the earliest pots bear the pseudo marks which were used from about 1760 to 1770. Invariably these pots were made of large capacity and were fitted with wooden handles for purposes of insulation. The first variations appeared about 1785, and we then note the introduction of the coffee jug. The primary difference between it and a pot is that a jug had a small spout soldered at the neck rather than a long curved pourer protruding from the belly. Many a one was fitted with a muslin bag which was placed directly inside the lip of the jug. Its purpose was to strain the coffee so that the grounds were not poured into the cup. Such jugs were often referred to as biggins and take their name from a colloquial word used in northern counties to describe a refreshment taken between meals. Baggin-time or Biggin-time was usually at ten o'clock in the morning or at four in the afternoon and represented a five-minute interlude from the day's work. A biggin was actually a container in the shape of a pot, having the capacity of a little more than a pint and often fitted with a deep removable lid or cover which could be used as a saucer. Many people today refer to the coffee pots which were mounted on stands with alcohol lamps as biggins, although it is safe to say that the earliest specimens were made as single units without the extra heating devices.

Chocolate Pots

Chocolate pots were known to have been produced, although in very few numbers. It is reasonable to assume that but a few households could indulge in the luxury of serving chocolate and, if they could, in all probability used containers made in solid silver.

Sugar Baskets

The high price and scarcity of sugar, no doubt, accounted for the very few containers that were made in Sheffield Plate. Although they appeared as early as 1770 in the shape of small baskets invariably fitted with blue glass liners, their production was limited; and it is for this reason that collectors are constantly seeking examples with the original crystals. Probably ninety percent of all that were made were pierced and the work they reflect is of high quality. Their relatively small size makes them readily adaptable to modern use. Indeed, it seems strange that these little sugar basins were never made to match services, and it would lead one to the general assumption that the tea imbibed by the English people was probably taken without benefit of sweetening. The sugar bowl seems to have been used as an individual unit more in the service of hot toddy than in the service of tea. It was generally placed on a tray along with nutmeg and other ingredients associated with the concoction of punch.

While one may encounter a limited number of these baskets, the appearance of a sugar dredger or shaker is almost unheard of. During the author's vast experience he has seen but a handful, and the assumption is that it was not thought practical to produce them in plate, since by this time they were plentiful in solid silver.

Cream Jugs

The name applied to the small containers for milk or cream was an apt one, for these jugs were miniatures of the larger specimens used in the service of wine. This is particularly true of the earliest examples. A typical one was mounted on a small round foot and fitted with a curved handle. Creamers dated from about 1778, although a few earlier types are available. We do not encounter any productivity in creamers until after the turn of the century when they were made in larger sizes and often as matching parts of tea services. At no time did the style of cream jugs assume the beauty of their counterparts in solid silver, and it seems as though the platers paid little attention to the production of these pieces.

Kettles

Only passing mention need be made of tea kettles, for they seem to be the neglected offspring of the Sheffield platers' family of endeavor. As a general rule it is difficult to encounter examples made prior to 1820. No doubt this is the reason that complete tea and coffee services are nearly impossible to assemble, for rarely were kettles made to match. It seems unfortunate that the early styles, of which a few were produced prior to 1800, are the most desirable ones, for they had a simplicity of design that is pleasing. The later types are usually set upon heavily embossed stands which detract greatly from their desirability.

Tea Urns

Containers for hot water in Sheffield Plate are known as early as 1765. The original ones were small, with a capacity from two to three quarts, and were beautiful specimens of fine proportion.

However, as the industry progressed, the size of the urns grew until shortly before the termination we find examples of gigantic capacity, far too richly embossed to be attractive. The later types were impractical, for their weight when filled with liquid was so great that it was well-nigh impossible to carry them. The majority of tea urns were made with no apparatus for keeping the contents hot, and had it not been for the introduction of an addition to accomplish this purpose, it is doubtful that they would have retained their popularity. The original method of heating was by the use of a piece of iron which, after having been placed in the stove, was inserted into a small metal container fitted to the inside of the urn. This, however, necessitated considerable work, first in heating the iron and then in depositing it safely in the body of the urn. Some were made with holders for charcoal. Although these methods were quite satisfactory, they were far from practical. With the introduction of the small alcohol lamp, which was placed directly beneath the base of the body, a really satisfactory solution was reached. However, the appearance of urns with alcohol lamps in Sheffield Plate is rare and for that reason specimens in original condition fetch very high prices today.

Tea Caddies

Although the original word "caddy" is taken from the Malayan "katé," which represented a unit of measurement, there seems to have been no hard or fast rule as applied to the sizes made by the Sheffield Platers. Caddies were made in great variations, and often the shape of their bodies would be homologous to the tea pots with which they were used. Many contained a partition to separate the black tea from the green and were fitted with a lock and key for the purpose of protection against pilferage. Caddies were among the earliest efforts of the platers, and are among the most sought-after articles for use in the modern home. While in America we do not greatly indulge in the service of tea, the caddy represents the perfect container for cigarettes, tobacco, or small biscuits. The most desired types are those with hinged covers because of their present-day adaptability. Those with pull-off covers are primarily serviceable for holding tea. We consider caddies among the most desirable of all articles made in Sheffield Plate.

Tea Machines

One of the most prodigious efforts of the platers was the tea machine. In effect it was the combination of three urns mounted on a base, and in all probability was used only in the homes of royalty. These articles are among the rarest known in Sheffield Plate, for they were expensive to produce and the market which received them was very limited. However, the idea incorporated in their use was extremely practical. The larger center urn was mounted on a swivel which permitted its spout to refill the two smaller ones. The purpose of the two urns was to hold the accepted different types of tea. Those privileged few who have ever owned a tea machine find their component parts are readily removable from the massive stand to allow individual use.

MISCELLANEOUS ARTICLES PRODUCED IN SHEFFIELD PLATE

A complete record of all the articles produced by the platers would be an impossible task. Many single specimens were manufactured of which we have no knowledge. However, we give below as complete a list of miscellaneous articles as can be gleaned from careful inspection of the records of the Sheffield Plate industry. No doubt the reader will look with amazement at many of these pieces, as they would hardly seem to come within the province of the manufacturers of plated ware. Nothing, however, seemed to daunt the workers in plate, and it seems as though they reveled in the thrill of producing a completely new object.

We must always bear in mind that these workers constituted an industry from which they gained their living, and had there not been a market ready to accept their wares they would have decreased the scope of their work. Many of the following were produced in very small quantities, and specimens of these rarities have not come down to us today. In addition, we wish to state, definitely, that some reader may well be the possessor of a rare isolated example not mentioned here. However, one can easily ascertain whether or not it is a true Sheffield Plated piece by permitting an expert to examine it.

Barber Dishes	Drawer Handles
Biscuit Boxes	Ear Speculums
Butter Dishes	Egg Boilers
Cigar Boxes and Holders	Egg Cups
Coach Lamps	Ear Trumpets
Coins	Flasks
Corks	Honey Pots
Dish Crosses	Knife Rests

Knife Trays

Knitting Sheaths

Lamps

Maces

Marrow Spoons

Mutton Holders

Nutmeg Graters

Pipes

Pipe Lighters

Shells

Slop Basins

Sugar Crushers

Tea Balls

Tinder Boxes

Toasting Forks

Toast Racks

Trowels

Wax Jacks

Chapter Nine

History of Electroplating

❦

W HILE THE TRADE of Sheffield Plating is remembered as an artistic
effort that achieved near perfection over a period of years, the
industry of electroplating was the beginning of big business. The ware
might have been termed Birmingham Plate, for it was in this city that
it originated. Yet no one can question the aptness of the term "Victorian
Plate" for silver plated ware made by the process of electrolysis during
the period circa 1840–1900. The dates are almost exactly the same as Victoria's. And it is this ware, now achieving the dignity of antiquity, that
claims the collector's interest.

The effect of electroplating was similar to that of the introduction of
the automobile to an age which had long known only the use of horse
power. Overnight the entire process of Sheffield Plating was discarded,
to the extent that within a matter of five years only two or three firms
were still engaged in working on the old style. Electroplating was the
means by which the manufacturer could bring his products to the public
at large at a price that all could afford.

Although many consider the firm of Elkington and Company as masters and discoverers of the process, there is doubt as to the veracity of
this. However, that was the firm which first foresaw the practical possibilities, and bought up every available patent. As a result, no competitor
could produce the new ware without paying a substantial royalty. Actually, we must pay tribute to Dr. Smee, an electrician, who was the
first to conceive that the power of the galvanic battery could collect or
disperse the atoms of pure metal in solution, so that they might be

directed to cover the surface of a metallic preparation. In a small laboratory in his own home, Dr. Smee gave a practical demonstration of this to eighty attending scientists. Not one left the meeting with any doubt that he had seen the beginning of an industry whose effect would be world-wide. It was not until 1844, however, that the first practical machine which produced goods by the new process was invented. It was the brainchild of John Woolrich of Birmingham and was constructed by Messrs. Prime and Son. This was the first magnetic machine to deposit a precious metal and was in use for many years, until superseded by equipment of improved design.

Although Dr. Smee was the first scientist to illustrate the process of electroplating, there is doubt that the original machine could have been constructed had not the discovery of induction by Professor Faraday been applied. Perhaps one of the minor uses to which this invention was turned was plating, for Faraday's discovery of obtaining electricity from magnetism had a far-reaching effect in innumerable industries. Although Elkington and Company were not the actual discoverers of the process, they were responsible for the majority of improvements which led to its founding as an industry of importance. The new method permitted goods to be sold at unbelievably low prices; and, in addition, there was less labor involved in production than was ever the case in Sheffield Plate. The craftsmen in Birmingham eagerly flocked to the manufactory of Elkington and Company, for the new process provided full-scale employment for all of mechanical mind. However, the city of Sheffield housed many "die hards" who needed more than a measure of convincing as to the future of plating by electrolysis.

The process of plating as developed to our day is carried out along the following lines. A rather sizable vat lined with Portland cement is used. Into this tank is poured a solution of cyanide of potassium dissolved in distilled water. The dynamo for the current is designed especially for the process of electroplating and is generally of low voltage, with the positive pole being attached to the silver sheet and the negative pole carried to the article to be plated. Perhaps of the utmost importance is the necessity for cleanliness of the article, for a single speck of dust or grease or even a finger mark will cause an imperfection to appear on the finished surface. (When you see a piece of plated ware that shows through in a single spot, in all probability this flaw was caused by a fault in the cleanliness of the article before plating.) Several methods of cleaning and rinsing are then employed after which the article is ready for the plating tank. It is firmly attached to the copper wires which are suspended from a brass rod. When the electricity is turned on, minute particles pass through the solution, removing the silver from its original sheet and depositing it firmly on the article in question. The amount of plating to be deposited is regulated by the length of time that the article is allowed to remain in the plating vat. When the process has been completed, the article will be removed with a porcelain-like appearance, after which a thorough polishing is required. However, during the last ten years a new process has been introduced by which the article is completely free of any finish when withdrawn from the tank. This obviously cuts down the cost of manufacture, for it does away with the need of subsequent buffing.

In every phase of manufacturing, the process of plating by electrolysis overcame all of the hardships that had formerly been experienced by the Sheffield platers. There is no doubt that articles produced in electroplate are of more durable quality than those made by the old process, although our love of the rare will always attract collectors of Sheffield Plate.

Whereas the workers in Sheffield Plate relied upon the silversmiths of contemporary period for the designs of many articles they produced, the situation was completely reversed with regard to the production of electroplated wares. There is little doubt, as evidenced by the pieces we have inherited, that the silversmiths copied from the manufacturers of electroplate, assiduously, yet conservatively. Twenty years after the founding of the industry, electroplated articles had found such a warm reception from buyers in all walks of life, that the silversmiths were obliged to exercise extreme caution, lest there be no sale for their products. Due to the relatively high cost of the metal, pieces in solid silver in most instances were five to six times more costly than those in plate. However, it is not to be thought that quantities of silver were not marketed during the Victorian era, but rather it is in comparison with the amount of Victorian Plate produced that it seems so small.

The amount of fine silver plated ware produced between the years 1860 and 1900 is amazing, not only for its huge numbers, but also for the wide variety. The difficulties of manufacture that had formerly beset workers in fine metals were overcome by the never-ending scores of improvements that were contributed by the thousands engaged in the industry. There was no piece that seemed beyond their ability, as study of many of their creations will illustrate. The field of endeavor ranged from such monstrosities as full-scale pieces of furniture to miniatures of household silver.

The quality of the workmanship approached perfection, and electroplate silver achieved enormous popularity. People were not satisfied with only the standard articles. They wanted more and more things in electroplate. This naturally led to the production of pieces which did little credit to the industry. Many were severely overornamented, and in size were hardly usable. Yet as an expression of wealth for those who had formerly been unable to partake of such luxuries, they were much sought after, and people did not hesitate to purchase pieces of lesser quality. Unfortunately the Victorian era in its closing period was the parent to one of the worst debacles in art the world has ever known.

By the year 1880, there were so many firms engaged in the industry that the trade began to suffer from overkeen competition. In their desire to create trade, many of the firms felt that unless they produced something new and different, they would be unable to make inroads into competitors' fields. This led to some very unusual wares, about which the less said the better. Had the firms been willing to reproduce pieces from the past century, the world would have inherited an untold amount of fine plate. But with the means of production on a relatively simple basis, many felt they had to use every tool and device at hand.

Extreme caution should be the byword in the purchase of pieces made during this period. It does require a careful eye to separate the wheat from the chaff, but there are many desirable articles available. One must also judge from the standpoint of use in the home of today, although it is safe to say that ninety percent of all made would find a proper place in modern living. There is much of elaborate design that is beautiful and worthy of ownership, as one will see by inspection of Victorian Plate. At any rate, one is assured of pieces of the highest quality of construction, regardless of the appeal of the styling.

To list all the articles made during the Victorian era would be practically impossible, for the period fostered a multitudinous array of unusual bits. However, in addition to the normal household objects that are readily and frequently seen, we are tabulating as many of the unusual as come to mind. The following are the contributions introduced by the platers during the Victorian era:

Alcohol Burning Table Lighters
Asparagus Dishes
Berry Dishes with Sugars and Creamers
Breakfast Condiment Sets
Café au lait Pots
Complete Tea and Coffee Services with Matching Trays
Compotes
Cracker Boxes
Crumb Scoops
Crystal Claret Jugs with Silver and Plated Mounts
Egg Boilers with Lamps
Flower Vases
Folding Biscuit Boxes
Hors d'oeuvre Dishes
Hot Plate Stands
Nests of Waiters
Pepper Grinders
Pickle Jars
Picture Frames
Revolving Tureens
Revolving Butter Tureens
Sardine Dishes
Stamp Boxes
Sugars and Creamers in Racks
Syphon Stands
Tea Infusers
Triple Shell Dishes
Two-Piece Fish Sets

SNUFF BOX   c. 1750
Possibly by Boulsover

BISCUIT BOX   c. 1800

CONDIMENT SETS

CRUET STAND   c. 1785
Thomas Watson & Co.

ONE OF A PAIR OF RARE SHEFFIELD PLATE
WARMING BOXES   c. 1790

CRUET STAND   c. 1810

PEPPER POT   c. 1780

Courtesy of S. Wyler, Inc.

*Courtesy of Harman & Co., Ltd.,
London*

DRINKING ARTICLES

THREE TANKARDS   c. 1770–1785

GOBLET   c. 1760

Courtesy of The Metropolitan Museum of Art

Courtesy of S. Wyler, Inc.

Courtesy of The Victoria and Albert Museum

EWER C. 1790

Courtesy of J. E. Caldwell & Co.

DECANTER STAND C. 1820

Courtesy of J. E. Caldwell & Co.

WINE FUNNEL C. 1815

WINE WAGON C. 1820

Courtesy of J. E. Caldwell & Co.

Courtesy of The Sussex Goldsmiths and Silversmiths Co., Ltd.,
Brighton, England

WINE COOLER   c. 1800

Courtesy of J. E. Caldwell & Co.

ICE PAIL   c. 1800

WINE COOLER   c. 1800

WINE COOLER   c. 1810

Courtesy of Harman & Co., Ltd., London

Courtesy of S. Wyler, Inc.

Courtesy of S. Wyler, Inc.

WINE COOLER WITH COVER c. 1815

Courtesy of Spink & Son, Ltd., London

WINE COOLER c. 1800

WINE COOLER c. 1818
Nathaniel Smith & Co.

WINE COOLER c. 1830

WINE COOLER c. 1835

Courtesy of Harman & Co., Ltd., London

Courtesy of J. E. Caldwell & Co.

Courtesy of S. Wyler, Inc.

IVORY-HANDLED DESSERT SERVICE   c. 1800
Close Plated

INKSTAND   c. 1780

INKSTAND WITH TELESCOPIC CANDLESTICK   c. 1790

GLOBE INKSTAND   c. 1790
Roberts, Cadman & Co.

INKSTAND C. 1810   *Courtesy of The Metropolitan Museum of Art*

INKSTAND C. 1800   *Courtesy of S. Wyler, Inc.*

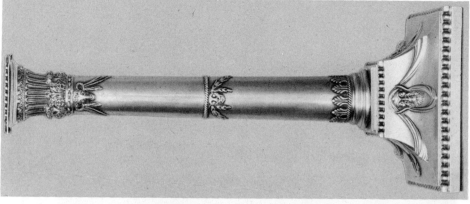

Courtesy of J. E. Caldwell & Co.
CANDLESTICK c. 1775
Thomas Law

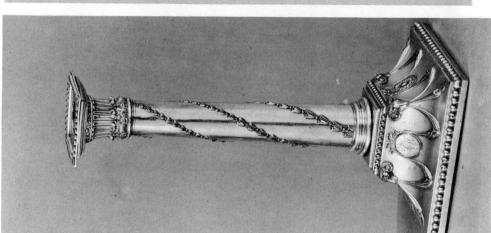

Courtesy of The Victoria and Albert Museum
CANDLESTICK c. 1780

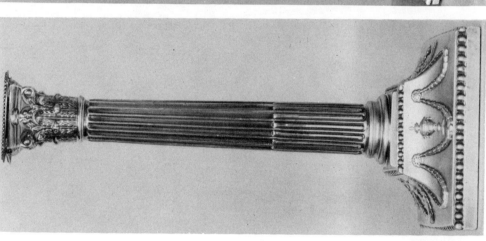

Courtesy of J. E. Caldwell & Co.
CANDLESTICK c. 1778
Matthew Fenton & Co.

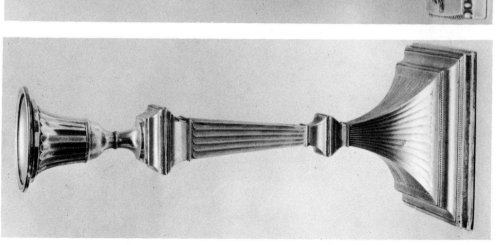

Courtesy of S. Wyler, Inc.
CANDLESTICK c. 1775

Courtesy of J. E. Caldwell & Co.
TELESCOPIC CANDLESTICK
c. 1815

Courtesy of S. Wyler, Inc.
CANDLESTICK   c. 1815

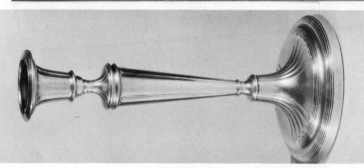

Courtesy of Spink & Son, Ltd.,
London
CANDLESTICK   c. 1790

Courtesy of J. E. Caldwell & Co.
CANDLESTICK   c. 1795
D. Holy Wilkinson

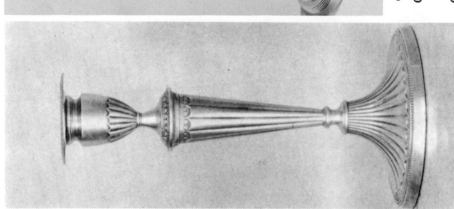

Courtesy of J. E. Caldwell & Co.
CANDLESTICK   c. 1785
J. Parsons & Co.

CANDELABRUM c. 1785

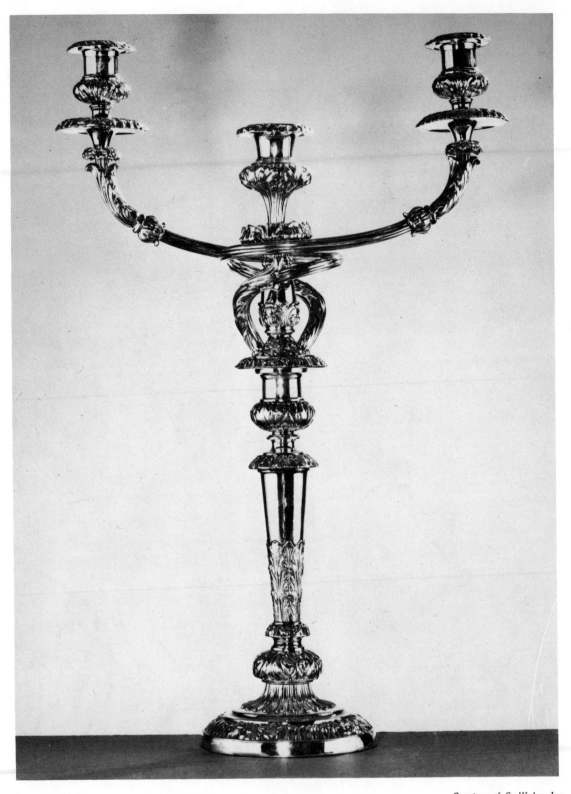

CANDELABRUM   c. 1820   Matthew Boulton

Courtesy of Walter H. Willson, Ltd., London

CANDELABRUM c. 1780
Thomas Law

Courtesy of Walter H. Willson, Ltd., London

CANDELABRUM WITH ONE OF FOUR
MATCHING CANDLESTICKS c. 1800
Matthew Boulton

*Courtesy of The Sussex Goldsmiths and Silversmiths
Co., Ltd., Brighton, England*

CANDELABRUM c. 1830

Courtesy of Asprey & Co., Ltd., London

CANDELABRUM AND CANDLESTICK
c. 1810

SUITE OF MATCHING CANDELABRA, URN AND PR. WINE COOLERS C. 1810

Courtesy of The Metropolitan Museum of Art
WALL SCONCE   C. 1790

Courtesy of J. E. Caldwell & Co.
CHAMBERSTICK AND SNUFFER   C. 1805   Nathaniel Smith & Co.

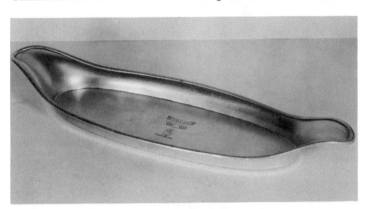

Courtesy of S. Wyler, Inc.
CHAMBERSTICK AND SNUFFER   C. 1810

Courtesy of J. E. Caldwell & Co.
SNUFFER TRAY   C. 1790

Courtesy of S. Wyler, Inc.
THREE WAX JACKS   C. 1780–1800

Courtesy of The Metropolitan Museum of Art
LAMP   C. 1790

TEA TRAY c. 1810
Watson and Bradbury

Courtesy of J. E. Caldwell & Co.

TEA TRAY c. 1830

Courtesy of J. E. Caldwell & Co.

Courtesy of S. Wyler, Inc.

WAITER c. 1765

Courtesy of S. Wyler, Inc.

WAITER c. 1815

Courtesy of S. Wyler, Inc.

TWO MATCHING WAITERS c. 1820

Courtesy of J. E. Caldwell & Co.

WAITER c. 1820
T. & J. Creswick

SUPPER SERVICE   c. 1825

CAKE BASKET   C. 1800

Courtesy of Spink & Son, Ltd., London

Courtesy of S. Wyler, Inc.

SWEETMEAT BASKET   C. 1770

Courtesy of S. Wyler, Inc.

BASKET   C. 1825

Courtesy of J. E. Caldwell & Co.

CHEESE DISH   c. 1820

Courtesy of S. Wyler, Inc.

FOUR CHEESE DISHES   c. 1800–1810

Courtesy of J. E. Caldwell & Co.

ENTREE DISH   c. 1820

Courtesy of The Metropolitan Museum of Art
DISH RING   c. 1775
Tudor and Leader

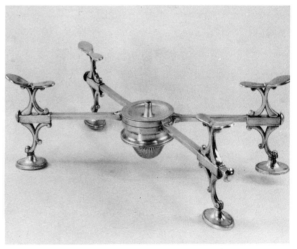

Courtesy of J. E. Caldwell & Co.
DISH CROSS   c. 1790

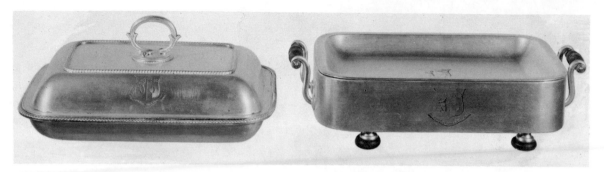

ENTREE DISH WITH WARMER C. 1800

Courtesy of S. Wyler, Inc.

Courtesy of The Sussex Goldsmiths and Silversmiths Co., Ltd.,
Brighton, England

ENTREE DISH C. 1805
Watson and Bradbury

Courtesy of Harman & Co., Ltd., London

ENTREE DISH C. 1810

THREE ENTREE DISHES C. 1825

Courtesy of The Sussex Goldsmiths and Silversmiths Co., Ltd., Brighton, England

Courtesy of S. Wyler, Inc.

EPERGNE AND PLATEAU   C. 1800

Courtesy of Harman & Co., Ltd., London

EPERGNE   C. 1790

REVOLVING WIREWORK EPERGNE

C. 1790   Richard Morton & Co.

Courtesy of The Sussex Goldsmiths and Silversmiths Co., Ltd., Brighton, England

Courtesy of Harman & Co., Ltd., London

EPERGNE c. 1800

*Courtesy of The Sussex Goldsmiths and Silversmiths Co., Ltd.,
Brighton, England*

EPERGNE WITH WATERFORD CRYSTAL DISHES
c. 1825

EPERGNE   c. 1820

Courtesy of S. Wyler, Inc.

Courtesy of S. Wyler, Inc.

SAUCE BOAT   c. 1770

Courtesy of Spink & Son, Ltd., London

SAUCE TUREEN   c. 1800

Courtesy of Harman & Co., Ltd., London

SAUCE BOAT   c. 1780

Courtesy of S. Wyler, Inc.

SAUCE TUREEN ON TRAY   c. 1815

Courtesy of Asprey & Co., Ltd., London

SAUCE TUREEN   c. 1810

SOUP TUREENS

SOUP TUREEN c. 1800
Courtesy of J. E. Caldwell & Co.

SOUP TUREEN c. 1810
Courtesy of S. Wyler, Inc.

SOUP TUREEN c. 1820
*Courtesy of The Victoria and
Albert Museum*

Courtesy of J. E. Caldwell & Co.

SOUP TUREEN c, 1815

Courtesy of S. Wyler, Inc.

SOUP TUREEN c. 1815

SOUP TUREEN   c. 1820

MISCELLANEOUS SERVICES

PART DINNER SERVICE   c. 1820   T. & J. Creswick

WARWICK VASE   c. 1780

SHEFFIELD PLATE TEA TRAY   c. 1815

PLATTER AND COVER   c. 1815

CHOP PLATTER   c. 1815
T. & J. Creswick

Courtesy of The Sussex Goldsmiths and Silversmiths Co., Ltd., Brighton, England

TEA POT AND STAND c. 1770

TEA POT c. 1785

Courtesy of Marshall Field & Co.

MATCHED TEA AND COFFEE SERVICE   C. 1800

Courtesy of The Sussex Goldsmiths and Silversmiths Co., Ltd., Brighton, England

FOUR-PIECE TEA SERVICE   c. 1805   D. Holy Parker & Co.

Courtesy of The Sussex Goldsmiths and Silversmiths Co., Ltd., Brighton, England

FOUR PIECE TEA SERVICE   c. 1825

Courtesy of The Victoria and Albert Museum

COFFEE POT c. 1765

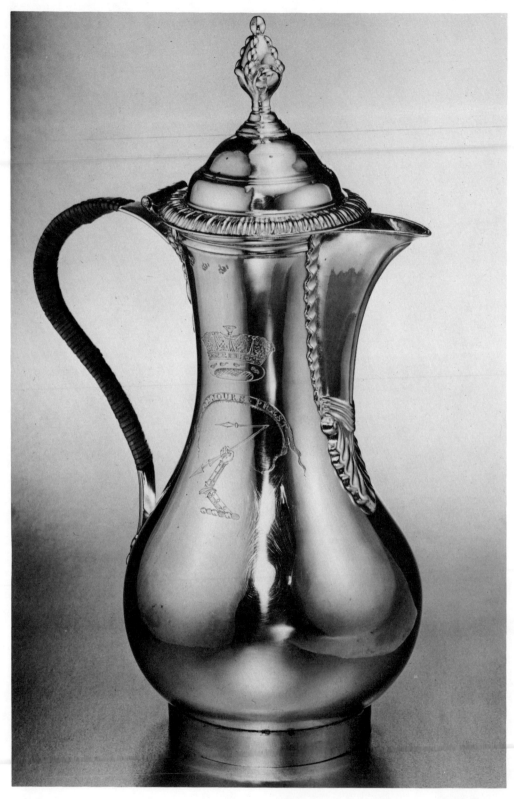

Courtesy of Marshall Field & Co.

COFFEE JUG (Showing Pseudo Hallmarks) c. 1760

COFFEE POT   c. 1760
Courtesy of S. Wyler, Inc.

Courtesy of Walter H. Willson, Ltd., London
COFFEE POT   c. 1765

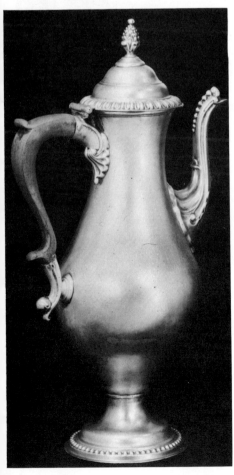

COFFEE POT   c. 1770
Courtesy of S. Wyler, Inc.

Courtesy of The Sussex Goldsmiths and Silversmiths Co., Ltd.,

MINIATURE TEA AND COFFEE SERVICE   c. 1790

Courtesy of S. Wyler, Inc.

BREAKFAST COFFEE POT   c. 1800

Courtesy of S. Wyler, Inc.

COFFEE POT   c. 1800

Courtesy of Harman & Co., Ltd., London

COFFEE POT   c. 1820

Courtesy of Harman & Co., Ltd., London

COFFEE POT   c. 1760

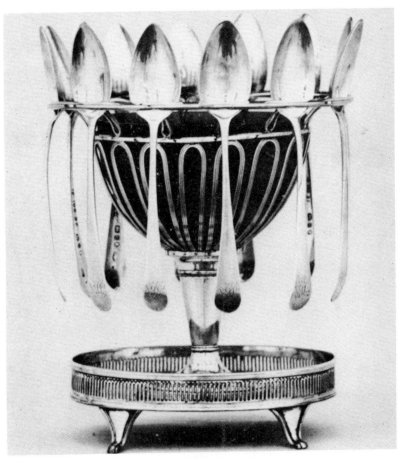

Courtesy of The Metropolitan Museum of Art

SUGAR BOWL WITH SILVER SPOONS   c. 1790
(Spoons, London, 1802: Thomas Wallis)

Courtesy of Harman & Co., Ltd., London

SUGAR BOWL AND CREAMER   c. 1815

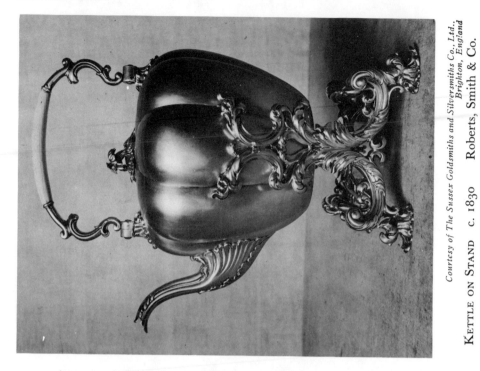

KETTLE ON STAND   C. 1830   Roberts, Smith & Co.

TEA KETTLE   C. 1830

COFFEE URN c. 1810

Courtesy of Marshall Field & Co.

Courtesy of Asprey & Co., Ltd., London

COFFEE URN C. 1810

Courtesy of J. E. Caldwell & Co.

COFFEE URN C. 1790

Courtesy of J. E. Caldwell & Co.

COFFEE URN C. 1800

Courtesy of Asprey & Co., Ltd . London

COFFEE URN C. 1785

Courtesy of Harman & Co., Ltd., London

COFFEE URN c. 1780

Courtesy of S. Wyler, Inc.

COFFEE URN c. 1795

Courtesy of S. Wyler, Inc.

THREE COFFEE URNS c. 1800–1825

COFFEE URN c. 1825

COFFEE URN c. 1815

Courtesy of S. Wyler, Inc.

COFFEE URN   c. 1800

Courtesy of S. Wyler, Inc.

COFFEE URN   c. 1815

Courtesy of Asprey & Co., Ltd., London

COFFEE URN   c. 1825

Courtesy of The Sussex Goldsmiths and Silversmiths Co., Ltd., Brighton, England

COFFEE URN   c. 1825

Courtesy of The Sussex Goldsmiths and Silversmiths Co., Ltd., Brighton, England

PR. TEA CADDIES WITH MATCHING SUGAR VASE AND COVER   c. 1790   Matthew Fenton & Co.

Courtesy of The Metropolitan Museum of Art

TEA CADDY   c. 1800

Courtesy of S. Wyler, Inc.

TEA CADDY   c. 1785

TEA CADDIES

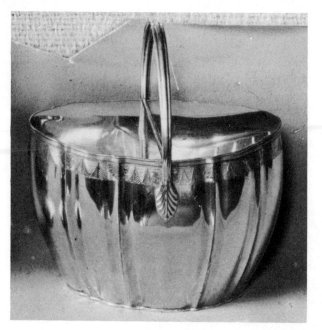

TEA CADDY c. 1790

TEA CADDY c. 1810

MISCELLANEOUS ARTICLES

CRIBBAGE BOARD (Very Rare) c. 1800

Courtesy of The Sussex Goldsmiths and Silversmiths Co., Ltd., Brighton, England

SELECTION OF PIERCED WORK C. 1770–1780

Courtesy of The Victoria and Albert Museum
CUP AND COVER   c. 1780

Courtesy of S. Wyler, Inc.
CHESTNUT VASE AND COVER   c. 1820

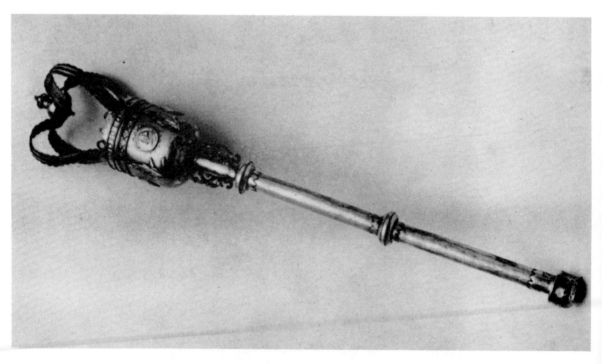

Courtesy of S. Wyler, Inc.

MACE (Very Rare)   c. 1765

Victorian
Plate

BUFFET TABLE WITH VICTORIAN ENGLISH PLATE

VICTORIAN PLATE COMPLETE TEA SERVICE AND TRAY   c. 1870   Elkington & Co.

Courtesy of S. Wyler, Inc.

ASSORTED VICTORIAN PLATE SERVERS   c. 1860–1885

Courtesy of S. Wyler, Inc.

VICTORIAN PLATE TEA SERVICE   c. 1880   Martin Hall & Co.
VICTORIAN PLATE GALLERY TRAY   c. 1880   Walker & Hall

VICTORIAN PLATE TUREEN ON PLATEAU   c. 1870
Elkington & Co.

VICTORIAN PLATE REVOLVING TUREEN   c. 1875

VICTORIAN PLATE ENTREE DISH   c. 1875

VICTORIAN PLATE c. 1850–1890
PR. CANDLESTICKS—TRIPLE SHELL—FOLDING BISCUIT BOX
TEA POT—TOAST RACK—CRUMB SCOOP

VICTORIAN PLATE   c. 1860–1880

Courtesy of S. Wyler, Inc.

EGG CRUET—WAITER—REVOLVING TUREEN   SOUP LADLE—CHEESE DISH

Courtesy of Museum Silver Shop, Inc.

VICTORIAN PLATE SUPPER SERVICE OR LAZY SUSAN   c. 1885

Victorian Plate Tea Caddy   c. 1870

Victorian Plate Egg Cruet   c. 1885

Victorian Plate: Set of 4 Candlesticks   c. 1885   Hawksworth, Eyre & Co.

Set of 3 Matched Waiters   c. 1875   Elkington & Co.

Chapter Ten

Identification of Originals and Recognition
of Spurious Pieces

❦

I F ONE WERE to place three objects of identical design in a row—one of solid silver, the next of Sheffield Plate and the last of electroplate— it would be difficult to tell them apart. The general appearance of all would be so similar that to the casual observer they would all seem to be of similar texture. The easiest distinction to make would be to identify solid silver from plate, for this could be done by the simple process of testing with acid. Inasmuch as we often encounter pieces bearing no mark whatsoever, it is not unusual to find file marks that have been applied by dealers in an attempt to ascertain the metallic content of the article in question. In order to be perfectly sure of the test, it is necessary to file through a definite outer layer of the part to be assayed, for some plated ware carries such a heavy coating of silver that a mere scratch mark would not penetrate to the base metal. The application of nitric acid on the bare spot will reveal immediately whether or not the piece is silver, for if the acid should bubble and turn green we have positive proof that the piece contains a base of metal other than silver. Of course, if the article has a set of hallmarks, it can readily be placed in its proper category if one knows the correct identification of the insignia. A further test sometimes employed is that of sound, for if one strikes a piece of real silver with a hard metal object it will have a certain resonance that is lacking in plated ware. In addition, silver is more malleable than plate and will be inclined to yield to pressure, whereas pieces of base metal construction will remain constantly firm.

The greatest difficulty is encountered in trying to recognize Sheffield

Plate correctly and authentically. Those who are experts in the field are prone to judge the age of a piece of silver or plate first from its color, for silver in particular, through the many processes of cleaning and oxidizing, assumes a patina. This may be better described as a softness of look that would normally be lacking in a reproduction. Although this test is reasonably sure, it is by no means the way for a layman to judge, for clever silversmiths can recolor a piece to simulate the old.

We know that Sheffield Plate was constructed in an entirely different manner from electroplate, and it is by examination of this now obsolete process that we are able to state with proper assurance the classification into which a piece may be placed. As we discussed in a previous chapter, pieces of original Sheffield Plate were joined together in such a manner as to exhibit a seam. If one carefully inspects an original he will find this seam by blowing his breath on the object, and as the cloud of moisture disappears, the seam will readily be apparent. This method of production has never been used in the manufacture of electroplated ware, for today all articles are made by the use of machinery which completely obliterates seaming. However, we may go still further and upon cursory examination view the application of the mounts. While many pieces of original plate are identified by the presence of silver edges, this again is not an infallible test, for certain unscrupulous manufacturers are so well versed in their trade that they are able to deposit not only silver borders but tin backs as well. The manner in which these backs and edges are applied, however, is often in a measure some proof, for whereas the reproductions are evenly soldered, those which are found on originals show the use of handcraft and lack of perfection. It is fairly safe to assume that many pieces bearing inlaid silver shields would be of the period, for rarely does one encounter a recent product bearing these.

There are fewer imitations of genuine Sheffield Plate manufactured for the purpose of deception than one would imagine. The reason for this is that the process of construction by the old method would entail an expense so great that the pseudo article would cost relatively as much as the original. As a general rule, it is through the ignorance of the seller that electroplated ware of the Victorian period is offered as Sheffield Plate. The author recently overheard a conversation wherein a dealer when asked the exact age of a piece replied that it was somewhere between fifty and one hundred and fifty years old. He further remarked that that should make little difference to the buyer, as the piece was attractive and reasonable. There is probably no worse way of antagonizing one's future trade than by the unwillingness to answer a logical query with an intelligent reply. To those readers who apply the knowledge they have gained from studying the industry, there will come a feeling of indignation at not being told the truth. This will be particularly true as they attain the status of being reasonably able to identify the genuine from the spurious. There are hundreds who prey upon the public's smattering of knowledge. If a piece is in a state of bleeding, they will claim it to be an original because of the copper base. We know now that nothing can be further from the truth, for the presence of a base metal is not the significant factor in determining the authenticity of Sheffield Plate.

If prospective buyers will bear in mind that a lack of knowledge is not a crime of which to be ashamed and will trade with honest vendors, rarely will they be the victims of misrepresentation. The average owner of a well-run establishment is only too eager to interest clients by explaining to them how he identifies originals. Inasmuch as he has at his beck and call the objects by which he can illustrate the particular points, he will be able to do this with little effort. Further, he will have interested future collectors in something fine, and nine times out of ten his patience will be well repaid by subsequent sales.

Through the years, there are few pieces that have not at sometime or other been attempted as simulations of fine originals. Many of these are not difficult to produce and for that reason one must always exercise keen judgment in buying. There are many tricks that are known to the unscrupulous that are worked on would-be purchasers daily. These always follow a pattern of similarity that is at all times disturbing and the cause of distrust. It is far safer not to inquire for the impossible and expect it to be offered within a matter of weeks, for it is often through a customer's insistence that a dealer feels obligated to produce a piece of spurious nature. In other words, if your home is well filled with fine originals do not be displeased if upon demanding a set of eight Sheffield Plate cigarette holders, you are told they are nonexistent. Your dealer is merely being honest and will in all probability suggest the use of an available article of the period for this purpose. Although it may not be perfectly adaptable, you will have the assurance of its being genuine, while elsewhere you may be offered reproductions in a poor state which will be sold to you as originals. If any doubt exists in your mind as to the authenticity of an article, it would be well to consult a volume such as this to find out whether or not pieces of this nature were ever included among the efforts of the platers.

Chapter Eleven

The Collecting of Sheffield Plate

❦

W HILE the term "collector" is frequently used with reference to art in many of its phases, it is indeed rare to find a person who by all standards qualifies for the title. Although those people who are outside the realm of the business world are prone to consider themselves collectors, if through their efforts they have assembled a group of objects, we in the trade would hardly put them in this category. In the opinion of the dealer, a collector is more of a student than a buyer, and, therefore, the term is not frequently applied. Let us say that it would be far better to describe those of wealth who have amassed worthwhile collections as patrons. There are unfortunately too few who have applied themselves intensively to a keen study in their particular field of collecting. In all probability this is due to a lack of time, for no better teacher can be found than experience.

To engage successfully in the collection of a particular aspect of art, it would be helpful to serve an apprenticeship, for it is through the knowledge of those who are learned in the field that one gains invaluable aid. Invariably the desire to accumulate too quickly is the cause of eventual disappointment. The true collector will follow a definite pattern in his search, and we feel that the following hints should prove valuable to those who are beginning.

Primarily, you must decide what you wish to collect. The same knowledge and instinct must be applied, whether you are interested in milk glass or fine pictures, for it is the desire to own rare specimens that identifies a connoisseur. Strangely, one does not suddenly decide that he is going to collect; it is usually a gradual process of awakening interest.

Some particular field will attract you to the extent that you will want to know more about it, and it is through the contacts of learning that the collector's instinct is born. However, it would be well to select a project that is not only possible from the standpoint of rarity, but also one that can be afforded. There is no item so insignificant that it can be regarded with disdain, for invariably an appreciation of the labor that went into the production of the piece at the time of its manufacture will be a stimulant. Although we do not regard all art with respect, we do pay homage to the ability of the majority of bygone craftsmen. Once your interest has been centered, you are ready for the next step in the process of collecting.

The quest for knowledge is of the utmost importance, for it is only through knowledge that one can learn to distinguish between the desirable and the commonplace. A great deal of learning may be gotten from textbooks that have been written on the subject of your interest, and careful perusal of these will be of great benefit. However, book learning alone is not enough, for it is through the actual handling of pieces that the finer points will be indelibly stamped in the mind. Perhaps the easiest way to accomplish this purpose is by frequent visits to shops wherein one is permitted to browse. The average dealer is only too willing to give assistance. It is through this type of customer relationship that a pleasant association is built. Perhaps, also, you may be fortunate enough to be granted the privilege of examining other collections either in museums or private homes. Every reconnaissance in the field will add further knowledge and you should grasp at every opportunity that presents itself.

Condition is a primary factor in the collection of anything that is old. Only those specimens which have weathered the ravages of hard usage should be sought after. As far as possible, exclude broken or repaired pieces. Their resale value will suffer sadly if at any time you wish to market them. Particularly in the fields of ceramics and crystal is this advice needed, for often clever workmen are able to repair broken parts so that the flaws are almost invisible to the naked eye. If you are interested in books you should thumb through the pages carefully; mutilation will immediately lessen the value. And so it is with all antiques; the present state of being must be regarded as the first inquiry.

We next turn to the problem of authenticity and it is here that you will be on your own to a great extent. Deal exclusively with firms who are well established and of good reputation. It is only through years of service and honest dealing that reputations such as these are earned. In the field of art a dealer must be regarded much in the same light as a family physician. The majority of good clients rely on their dealers for the true history of a piece. In the matter of authenticity you must rely on your studies, and if a piece seems to be out of period or if you are dubious as to its quality, it is best not to buy it without proper counsel and advice.

With regard to value, the subject is always open, since antiques in general have an intrinsic value that is difficult to define. For example, if one owns a piece which is an isolated example of its type, he is privileged to ask any amount, for there is no competition. Yet values such as these are governed by the law of supply and demand and eventually fall into a category that is both acceptable and fair. With respect to those pieces of which several are available one will generally find an established price. This may have been determined through the medium of auction or appraisal. Shops normally enjoy a percentage of profit which lends itself to respectability both from the standpoint of the dealer and the buyer.

The closing note with regard to collecting must include this thought: If perchance in the early days of your endeavors you have purchased poor or unworthy examples, do not hesitate to discard them, even at a loss, for their inclusion in a proper collection will do little but slight the better pieces. Always remember that no one is infallible and the greatest experts in the world have made serious mistakes. However, study the error of your ways and you will not make the same mistake again.

All of the foregoing has been advice to collectors in general, and yet this book would not be complete if we did not discuss the collection of Sheffield Plate as a separate and distinct item. While the thoughts listed above are comparatively inclusive, in seeking an example of Sheffield Plate we must imbue ourselves with something more definite, for each field presents its own particular problems. Were we to state the one outstanding feature to be looked for, it would probably be condition. As we know, Sheffield Plate is a combination of the fusion of two metals which when submitted to hard wear would show signs of same. Therefore, it is only those items which are still in their original state of manufacture that we view with high regard. Undoubtedly, thousands upon thousands of original specimens of Sheffield Plate have over a period of years been subjected to replating by the process of electrolysis. This is quite understandable, for at the time of their manufacture Sheffield Plated articles were made for use and not for display. However, so many have been inherited that we can afford to pick and choose. A lack of patina will invariably denote that an article has been replated. The softness and mellowness that come with age would of a surety be lacking. In addition, one often finds evidence through the discovery of tiny bubbles on the surfaces wherein the new plate has not adhered properly to the original base metal. We should carefully inspect articles which were made with crystal containers. Those that are bereft of the linings with which they were made are to be discarded, for they are no longer, in the eye of the expert, original. The same may be said of handles and knobs, although we are not so likely to reject a prospective purchase because of a new handle.

In dealing with articles made of metal we frequently encounter the problems of addition and subtraction. Although this is most noticeable in the field of solid silver, it is sometimes seen on pieces of Sheffield Plate. The subject of addition is best exemplified in the following manner: a pair of Sheffield Plate candlesticks has added to it a pair of branches which will nearly match. This same case might again be seen in any type of open dish which has been fitted with a cover for the purpose of convenience, although it originally carried none. These additions detract immediately from the authenticity of the article and should not at any time be considered as worthy. The problem of subtraction is just the opposite, for herein one encounters an original piece which is minus some part. This is best noted with reference to a decanter or cruet stand which may have been equipped with four bottles or more to match, while at the present moment it is minus some of the originals. On this subject, we can state with more than a note of finality that no article, if not in original condition, should be included in a proper collection.

We have learned that Sheffield Plate can be recognized by the presence of seams as well as by silver shields and turned-over silver edges.

If the piece in question is of a period where seams were used, it would be well to look for them, as they would clearly indicate authenticity.

In conclusion, in the selection of specimen pieces one should bear in mind that articles made during the different stages of the industry varied greatly. Therefore, it would be of the utmost interest to collect, if possible, succeeding specimens of the same object, for in this way the improvements would be readily apparent. While one's normal taste might run to the simpler styles, those of extravagant ornamentation were masterpieces of workmanship and should be included in any representation of the industry. The collecting of old plate is a worthy task, for certain articles are practically non-existent and yet it is the acquisition of these that truly thrills the collector. However, the greatest virtue must be patience, and often one will spend years seeking a rare example. It is this sustaining interest which will do much to enlarge the field of those interested in Sheffield Plate. There is extreme pleasure in seeking good examples, for there are so many that are unworthy. Yet, it will be your own ability, gained from countless experiences, that will help you eliminate the unwanted.

To those of you who are interested—Happy Hunting!

Chapter Twelve

The Care and Cleaning of Sheffield Plate

❦

ALTHOUGH THE component elements that constitute Sheffield Plate are metals of great durability, the wearing qualities of the completed product are definitely of a fragile nature. This combination of silver and copper which has been achieved through a process of fusion tends, unfortunately, to have great erosive qualities unless properly cared for. No matter how heavily plated an article may be, the various layers of silver will eventually wear off. Inasmuch as we know that Sheffield Plate tarnishes and for that reason requires constant polishing, it is of vast importance to treat articles in this category with great delicacy. For this reason we shall dwell for a moment on the recommended processes for cleaning.

There are available today any number of good silver polishes, the majority of which are composed of a base of whiting. This is a product in white powder form, possessing no harmful qualities, which lends itself admirably to the removal of tarnish. In many homes in England, a combination of whiting and plain water with a touch of rouge is all that is used, even for the finest of old family plate. However, in this country we are the victims of advertising propaganda to the extent that we often buy those products that promise the impossible. Fortunately, there are few polishes on the market of liquid or paste content that are damaging. A sure test, however, would be to take a bit of the polish and rub it between one's thumb and forefinger until the substance has practically disappeared. If any minute gritty particles remain, it would be wise to avoid such a product, as these will act as an abrasive.

It is of the utmost importance in cleaning Sheffield Plate to use a polish that will not affect its patina. In other words, if the removal of tarnish were the sole object, one could easily immerse pieces in a solution of cyanide, and they would emerge completely cleaned. However, its characteristic coloring would then make the articles resemble aluminum or white metal, rather more than silver. It is for this reason that the author does not recommend acid or any electrical process in the cleaning of one's old silver or plate. However, let us suppose that one has purchased a piece of fine Sheffield Plate that is sadly in need of replating and that the resulting product has a look of polished chromium. The application of the fumes of a burning candle, plus the rubbing of ordinary rouge will do more to help restore the original color than anything else. If for any reason a candle is not available, lamp black may be substituted. If one encounters pieces that have not been cleaned for many years and are heavily encrusted with a tarnish that seems to defy the utmost of "elbow grease," it is advisable to add a few drops of ammonia to the particular polish that you are using. This will enable one to clean more easily and at the same time will not remove the silver from the copper base. The use of hot water will bring by far the best results plus rubbing with a chamois cloth for giving a high luster. Although the chore of cleaning silver is a laborious one, normal household plate should be attended to at least once a week, for by this timetable the work will be reduced to a minimum of effort.

One often hears the word "finish" applied to silver and it is well to be careful in regard to this. Whether one's silver is old or reproduction, the greatest beauty of the metal is its natural color. The softness of texture that is associated with silver can be enjoyed only when pieces are neither too dull nor too bright.

When the summer months approach and silver is to be stored for a period of time, it is wise to take every possible precaution to prevent it from tarnishing too greatly. There are available today tarnish-proof tissue paper and flannel bags, both of which are highly recommended. If the silver is to be deposited in an air-tight compartment such as a cabinet with a locked door, the use of camphor will in a measure prevent tarnish. Actually, it is the qualities that are in the air that cause silver to turn a brownish color. Were we able to remove all the sulphur in the atmosphere, silver would never tarnish. Since this is impossible, it is wise to undertake all of the known labor-saving devices available.

Many times people will refuse a fine piece with the remark that it is scratched. Always bear in mind that the item in question was made for use, and if it does not show signs of wear it could not possibly be in an "original" state.

Sheffield Plate Marks

Note: Sheffield Plate Marks are listed chronologically; an alphabetical index of makers is given here for the convenience of the reader.

Allgood J.
Allport E.
Ashforth G. & Co.
Askew
Atkin Henry

Banister W.
Beldon G.
Beldon, Hoyland & Co.
Best H.
Best & Wastidge
Bingley W.
Bishop Thomas
Blagden, Hodgson & Co.
Boulton M. & Co.
Bradshaw J.
Briggs W.
Brittain, Wilkinson & Brownill
Butts T.

Causer J. F.
Cheston T.
Child T.
Coldwell W.
Colmore S.
Cope C. G.
Corn J. & J. Sheppard
Cracknall J.
Creswick T. & J.

Davis J.
Deakin, Smith & Co.
Dixon J. & Sons.
Dixon T. & Co.
Drabble I. & Co.
Dunn G. B.

Ellerby W.
Evans S.

Fox T. & Co.
Freeth H.
Froggatt, Coldwell & Lean

Gainsford R.
Garnett W.
Gibbs G.
Gilbert J.
Goodman, Gainsford & Fairbairn
Goodwin E.

Green J.
Green J. & Co.
Green W. & Co.

Hall Henry
Hall W.
Hanson M.
Harwood T.
Harrison G.
Harrison J.
Hatfield A.
Hill D. & Co.
Hinks J.
Hipkiss J.
Hipwood W.
Hobday J.
Holland H. & Co.
Holy D. & G.
Holy D., Parker & Co.
Holy D., Wilkinson & Co.
Horton D.
Horton J.
Howard S. & T.
Hutton W.

Jervis W.
Johnson J.
Jones
Jordan T.

Kirby S.

Law J. & Son
Law R.
Law T. & Co.
Lea A. C.
Lees G.
Lilly John
Lilly Joseph
Linwood J.
Linwood M. & Sons
Linwood W.
Love J. & Co.

Madin F. & Co.
Mappin Bros.
Markland W.
Meredith H.
Moore F.
Moore J.

Morton R. & Co.

Needham C.
Newbould W. & Son
Nicholds J.

Oldham T.

Padley, Parkin & Co.
Parsons J. & Co.
Peake
Pearson R.
Pemberton & Mitchell
Pimley S.
Prime J.

Roberts & Briggs
Roberts, Cadman & Co.
Roberts, J. & S.
Roberts, Smith & Co.
Rodgers J. & Sons
Rogers J.
Ryland W. & Son

Sansom T. & Sons
Scot W.
Shephard J.
Silk R.
Silkirk W.
Small T.
Smallwood J.
Smith & Co.
Smith I.
Smith J.
Smith J. & Son
Smith N. & Co.
Smith, Sissons & Co.
Smith, Tate, Nicholson & Hoult
Smith W.
Staniforth, Parkin & Co.
Stot B.
Sutcliffe R. & Co.
Sykes & Co.

Thomas S.
Thomason E. & Dowler
Tonks & Co.
Tonks Samuel
Tudor, Leader & Nicholson
Turley S.
Turton J.
Tyndall J.

Walker, Knowles & Co.
Waterhouse & Co.
Waterhouse George & Co.

Waterhouse, Hatfield & Co.
Waterhouse I. I. & Co.
Watson, Fenton & Bradbury
Watson J. & Son
Watson, Pass & Co.
Watson W.
White, J.
Wilkinson H. & Co.
Wilmore Joseph
Woodward W.
Worton S.
Wright J. & Fairbairn G.

Younge S. & C. & Co.

Name of Firm.	Maker's Marks.	Date.
Ashforth G. & Co. ...		1784
Fox T. & Co.	FOX, PROCTOR PASMORE & Cº	1784
Green W. & Co.	W. GREEN &Cº	1784
Holy D., Wilkinson & Co.	DANᵗ HOLY WILKINSON & Cº	1784
Law T. & Co.	THOˢ LAW & Cº	1784
Parsons J. & Co.	JOHN PARSONS & Cº	1784
Smith N. & Co.	N· SMITH & Cº	1784
Staniforth, Parkin & Co.	STANIFORTH PARKIN & Cº	1784
Sykes & Co.	SYKES & Cº	1784
Tudor, Leader & Nicholson	TUDOR & Cº	1784
Boulton M. & Co. ...	BOULTON	1784
Dixon T. & Co.	DIXON & Cº	1784
Holland H. & Co. ...	HOLLAND & Cº	1784
Moore J.	MOORE §	1784
Smith & Co.	SMITH & Cº	1784

Name of Firm.	Maker's Marks.	Date.	Name of Firm.	Maker's Marks.	Date.
Beldon, Hoyland & Co...		1785	Newbould W. & Son ...		1804
Brittain, Wilkinson & Brownill		1785	Drabble I. & Co. ...		1805
Deakin, Smith & Co.] ...		1785	Coldwell W.		1806
Love J. & Co. ... ... (Love, Silverside, Darby & Co.)		1785	Hill D. & Co, ...		1806
Morton R. & Co. ...		1785	Law J. & Son ...		1807
Roberts, Cadman & Co.		1785	Butts T.		1807
Roberts J. & S.		1786	Green J.		1807
Sutcliffe R. & Co. ...		1786	Hutton W.		1807
Bingley W.		1787	Law R.		1807
Madin F. & Co.		1788	Linwood J.		1807
Jervis W.		1789	Linwood W.		1807
Colmore S.		1790	Meredith H.		1807
Goodwin E. ...		1794	Peake		1807
Watson, Fenton & Bradbury		1795	Ryland W & Son ...		1807
Froggatt, Coldwell & Lean		1797	Scot W		1807
Green J. & Co.		1799	Silkirk W		1807
Goodman, Gainsford & Fairbairn		1800	Thomason E. & Dowler...		1807
Ellerby W.		1803			
Garnett W.		1803	Tonks Samuel		1807
Holy D., Parker & Co. ...		1804			

Name of Firm.	Maker's Marks.	Date.	Name of Firm.	Maker's Marks.	Date.
Waterhouse & Co. ...		1807	Hanson M.		1810
Wilmore Joseph ...		1807	Pimley S.		1810
Gainsford R.		1808	Creswick T. & J. ...		1811
			Stot B.		1811
Hatfield A.		1808	Watson, Pass & Co. (late J. Watson)		1811
Banister W.		1808	Lees G.		1811
Gibbs G.		1808	Pearson R.		1811
Hipkiss J.		1808	White J. (White & Allgood)		1811
Horton D.		1808	Kirkby S.		1812
Lea A. C.		1808	Allgood J		1812
Linwood M & Sons ...		1808	Allport E		1812
Nicholds J		1808	Gilbert J		1812
Beldon G.		1809	Hinks J.		1812
Wright J. & Fairbairn G.		1809	Johnson J		1812
Cheston T		1809	Small T		1812
Harrison J		1809	Smith W		1812
Hipwood W.		1809	Younge S. & C & Co. ...		1813
Horton J		1809	Thomas S.		1813
Silk R.		1809	Tyndall J		1813
Howard S. & T.		1809	Best H.		1814
Smith, Tate, Nicholson & Hoult		1810	Cracknall J.		1814
Dunn G B		1810	Jordan T.		1814

Name of Firm.	Maker's Marks.	Date.	Name of Firm.	Maker's Marks.	Date
Woodward W.		1814	Blagden, Hodgson & Co.		1821
Lilly John		1815	Holy D. & G.		1821
Best & Wastidge ...		1816	Needham C.		1821
Ashley		1816	Sansom T. & Sons ...		1821
Davis J.		1816	Child T.		1821
Evans S.		1816	Smith I.		1821
Freeth H.		1816	Worton S.		1821
Harwood T.		1816	Rodgers J. & Sons ...		1822
Lilly Joseph		1816			
Turley S.		1816	Bradshaw J.		1822
Cope C. G.		1817	Briggs W.		1823
Pemberton & Mitchell ...		1817	Harrison G.		1823
Shephard J.		1817	Smallwood J.		1823
			Causer J. F.		1824
Markland W.		1818	Jones		1824
			Tonks & Co.		1824
			Roberts, Smith & Co. ...		1828
Corn J. & J. Sheppard...		1819	Smith J. & Son		1828
Rogers J.		1819	Askew		1828
Hall W. ..., ...		1820	Hall Henry		1829
Moore F.		1820	Hobday J.		1829
Turton J.		1820	Watson J. & Son ...		1830

Name of Firm.	Maker's Marks.	Date.
Bishop Thomas... ...		1830
Hutton W.		1831
Atkin Henry		1833
Waterhouse I. & I. & Co.		1833
Watson W.	W. WATSON MAKER SHEFFIELD	1833
Dixon J. & Sons	DIXON'S IMPERIAL ... JAS. DIXON'S	1835
Smith J.	JOSEPHUS SMITH	1836
Waterhouse, Hatfield & Co.		1836
Wilkinson H. & Co. ...		1836
Hutton W.	Hutton Hutton	1837
Hutton W.	H & S	1839
Prime J.	PS	1839
Walker, Knowles & Co.		1840
Waterhouse George & Co.	W & Co S	1842
Smith, Sissons & Co. ...		1848
Padley, Parkin & Co. ...		1849

Name of Firm.	Maker's Marks.	Date.
Hutton W.	W H & S T	1849
Mappin Bros.	MAPPIN BROS	1850
Oldham T.	T. OLDHAM MAKER NOTTINGHAM	1860
Roberts & Briggs ...	R & B	1860

MISCELLANEOUS MARKS WHICH HAVE NOT BEEN TRACED.

Maker's Marks.	Approximate date of manufacture.
	1780-1790
BEST PLATE	1790
DEVER	1790
ALWH GA IH EF	1790-1800
Do.	1790-1800
R° JEWESSON MIDLETON & C° *	1800-1810
W.B. PINE 352 STRAND	1815-1825
	1815 1825
WILSON	1815-1825
GILBERT LONDON	1840
REGISTERED BY MAPPLEBECK & LOWE JAN 27 1840 N° 223	1840
RW&W	1840
PAT ENT PAT ENT	1840
	1850
SALT	1850
	1850
R O + GRC	1850

Allen, Edgar
and Company
Imperial Steel
Works
Sheffield

Allen and Martin
Birmingham

Aluminium
Company Ltd.
London

Archer and
Company
Sheffield

Archer, Machin
and Marsh
Sheffield

Armstrong,
Stevens, and Son
Birmingham

Army and Navy
Co-operative
Society, Ltd.
Westminster

Ashberry, Philip
and Sons
Sheffield

Aston, T. and Son
Birmingham

A&S

Atkin Brothers
Truro
Sheffield

A B ✳ S

HA FA FA

H.A

Atkin, Henry
Sheffield

H.A

Atkinson Brothers
Milton Works
Sheffield

Badger, T.
Sheffield

TB&C

Badger, Worrall
and Armitage
Sheffield

BW&A

Baker, John
and Company
Wheeldon Works
Sheffield

MERIT

Barker Brothers
Birmingham

GRIEL NICKEL SILVER

Barnascone, Lewis
Sheffield

Barnes, Frederick
and Company
*London,
Birmingham
and Sheffield*

Baum, Maurice
Sheffield

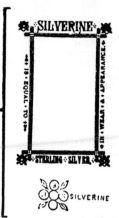

Batt, John
and Company
London

Beach and Minte
Birmingham

Beal, J. and J.
Redhill Works
Sheffield

Beal, M.
Sheffield

Beardshaw, A. J.
and Company
Sheffield

Bell, J. and J.
Sheffield

Bell, John
Sheffield

Bell, Jonathan
Sheffield

Benson, J. W.
London

Batt, William
and Sons
Sheffield

Biggin, John
Sheffield

Bingham
and Ogden
Sheffield

Bingley, George
Bower
Sheffield

WARRANTED
SILVER SOLDERED.

Binnall, R.
and Company
Shrewsbury

Birts and Son
Woolwich

WITHIN
THE REACH OF
ALL.

Bishop, George
and Sons
Sheffield

MITRE.

Blyde, John
Clintock Works
Sheffield

GENIUS.

Boardman, C.
Sheffield

CB

Boardman, Glossop
and Company
Clarence Works
Sheffield

Bolsover, Henry
Portland Works
Sheffield

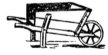

Bonser and Son
London

Box, W. R.
and Company
Dublin

SILVERSTEIN.

Bradbury, Thomas
and Sons
Sheffield

Bradley, Albert
Samuel
Sheffield

TOPAZ.

Bradley, E.
Sheffield

EB

Bramwell,
Brownhill
and Company
Sheffield

Brearley, W.
Sheffield

W B

Briddon Brothers
Victoria Plate
Works
Sheffield

B.B

AB
FB

Bright, S.
and Company
Sheffield

Brittain, S.
and Company
St. George's Works
Sheffield

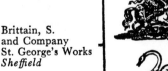

Brookes
and Crookes
Atlantic Works
Sheffield

B&C

Christofle
and Company
Paris

Clark, John
Birmingham

CLARKS

JUBILEE GOLD

Brooks, Henry
and Company
London

Collings and Wallis
Birmingham

MONTANA SILVER.

Collins, Charles
Howard
Birmingham

Browett, Alfred
Birmingham

Co-operative
Wholesale Society,
Ltd., The
Manchester

Browett, Ashberry
and Company
Birmingham

Copley, John
and Sons
Richmond Works
Sheffield

XX

Cowlishaw, J. Y.
Sheffield

Brown and Clark
Birmingham

B&C

Cowper-Coles,
Cowper Bickerton
London

ARCAS

Chantrill
and Company
Birmingham

Creswick
and Company
Sheffield

CRESWICK & C?

Charles, Andrew
Birmingham

HESSIN.

Charlton Brothers
Birmingham

Creswick, T. J.
and N.
Sheffield

Chesterman, James
and Company
Bow Works
Sheffield

Culf, Arthur
Sheffield

Cutts, J. P.
Sheffield

Daffern, William
Birmingham

RAENO

Daniel and Arter
Globe Nevada
Silver Works
Birmingham

NEVADA SILVER

LAXEY SILVER

INDIAN SILVER

BRAZILIAN SILVER

ALUMINIUM SILVER

BENGAL SILVER

JAPANESE SILVER

ARGENLINE

BURMAROID

Deakin, G.
and Company
Sheffield

Deakin, James
and Sons
Sheffield

Derby, John
and Sons
Sheffield

Derry, Frederick
Birmingham

"ROYAL STANDARD"

"ROYAL STANDARD"
VICTORIA
SILVER

 "STANDARD"
VICTORIA
SILVER

Dixon, James
and Sons
Sheffield

JD&S

Dodge, W. and M.
Manchester

Doughty,
Alexander
and Company
Liverpool

GUANACO

Drysdale,
Johnathan
and Josiah
and Company
London

GUANACO

Dyson, John
Leeds

Eaton, T. W.
Sheffield

Edwards, George
Glasgow

Eglington, F.
Staffordshire
 EGLENTINE

Elkington and
Company, Ltd.
Birmingham

ELKINGTON & C°

ELKINGTON

ELKINGTON
ELKINGTON & C°

Elkington, Mason
and Company
Birmingham
E M & C°

Ellis, Charles
and Company
Sheffield
C E & C°

Ellis, Isaac
and Sons
Sheffield
 ISAAC ELLIS & SONS. SHEFFIELD.

Ellis, T.
Plymouth

Elmore, John S.
and Company
London

Evans, Lescher,
and Webb
London
SAVARS.

Evans Sons
and Company
Liverpool
SAVARS.

Farrow
and Jackson
London
FARROW & JACKSON
LONDON & PARIS.

Fear, Edwin
Bristol

Fenton
and Anderton
Sheffield
F&A

Fenton Brothers
Sheffield
FBrs
JFF &FF

Fenton, J. F.
Sheffield
J·F·F

Fenton, James
Birmingham
JF

Field, Alfred
and Company
*Birmingham
and Sheffield*

G ✠ B

Fielding, Henry
Birmingham
SILVENE

Freeman, T.
Sheffield
TF

Gallimore, W.
and Company
Sheffield
W·G   WG

Gangee, John
The Glaciarium
Middlesex

Garfitt, Thomas
and Son
Cross Scythes
Works
Sheffield

Gilbert, Joseph
Sun Works
Birmingham

ALMADA SILVER

ARGENTINA SILVER

Joseph Gilbert

Gilbert and
Spurrier, Ltd.
Birmingham

Gilding
and Silvering
Company, The
Middlesex

ARGOSY SILVER

Glauert, L. and C.
Sheffield

"PATRIOT"

Goldsmiths'
Alliance, Ltd.
London

Goodall, Henry
Arthur
London

BB

Goode, John
and Sons
Birmingham

Gorer, Solomon
Lewis
Middlesex

Gotscher
and Company
Birmingham

Grayson, Benjamin
Sheffield

BRITISH

Green, J.
Sheffield

Grinsell and Sons
London

Hale Brothers
Sheffield

Hancock, Samuel
and Sons
Mazeppa Works
Sheffield

Hands, Thomas
Birmingham

ARGOSY SILVER

Hands and Sons
Birmingham

Harrison Brothers
and Howson
Sheffield

Harrison, J.
and Company
Norfolk Works
Sheffield

Harrison, J.
Sheffield

Harrison, W. W.
and Company
Montgomery Works
Sheffield

Hawksley, G.
Sheffield

Hawksley, G.
and Company
Sheffield

Hawksworth, Eyre
and Company
Sheffield

Hayman
and Company
Birmingham

SIBERIAN SILVER

SOLE PROPRIETORS

PERFECTION

SOLE PROPRIETORS

Heckford, Arthur
Egerton
Birmingham

Hills, Menke
and Company
Birmingham

AFRICAN SILVER

Hobson, Henry
and Sons
*London
and Sheffield*

Hodd, A. and Sons
Middlesex

Hope, J. V. and
Hope, G. F. W.
Atlantic Works
*Wednesbury
and London*

Howard, Francis
Aberdeen Works
Sheffield

Howarth, James
and Sons
Sheffield

Howell and
James, Ltd.
London

*The "Sceptre
"Jubilee"*

Hukin and Fenton
Sheffield

Hukin and Heath
Birmingham

Humphreys, W. R.
and Company
Sheffield

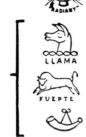

Hunter, Michael
and Son
Talbot Works
Sheffield

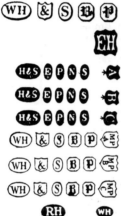

Hutton, William
and Sons
*Sheffield
and London*

Ibberson, George
Sheffield

Ihlee and Horne
London

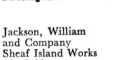

Ingram, John
Birmingham

Jackson, William
and Company
Sheaf Island Works
Sheffield

James, John
and Sons
Victoria Works
Redditch

LEVIATHAN.

Johnson, R. M.
and Company
Shoreham Plate
Works
Sheffield

Jones, C.
Liverpool

PILOT

Judd and Company
London

THE CYPRUS

Keep Brothers
Birmingham

Knight, Henry
and Company
London

Knowles, J.
and Son
Sheffield

Koerber
and Company
London

Lander, Edwin
and Company
Birmingham

 GLORIOUS.

Lee, William
and Sons
Sheffield

Lee and Middleton
Sheffield

Lee and Wigfull
John Street Works
Sheffield

ALBION SILVER

Lever Brothers
Port Sunlight

SUNLIGHT

Levesley Brothers
Central Works
Sheffield

Levetus Brothers
Birmingham

A PERFECT
IMITATION OF FINE GOLD.

"KARANTI SILVER"

GOLDTECTA

"ECLIPSE SOVEREIGN PURSE

Levy Brothers
London

Levy, M. de J.
and Sons
London

Lloyd, Taylor
and Company
London

Lockwood
Brothers, Ltd.
Sheffield

Long, Hawksley
and Company
Hallamshire Works
Sheffield

Lowe, T. P.
Sheffield

MacKay
and Chisholm
Edinburgh

McClelland,
James Robert
Sheffield

McDonald
and Company
*Birmingham
and Whitby*

McEwan, James
and Company
Ltd.
London

McLean Brothers
and Rigg, Ltd.
London

McMurtrie, John
McLeownan
Glasgow

Maigatter, Carl
London

Makin, E. J.
Sheffield

Mammatt, Buxton
and Company
Arundel Plate
Works
Sheffield

Manton, J. S.
and Company
Birmingham

Mappin Brothers
Queens Works
*Sheffield
and London*

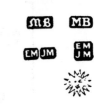

Mappin and
Company
Royal Cutlery
Works
Sheffield

Mappin, Joseph
and Brothers
Sheffield

Mappin and Son
Sheffield

Mappin, Webb
and Company
Sheffield

Mappin and Webb
Royal Cutlery
Works
*Sheffield
and London*

Marples, T.
Sheffield

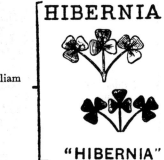

HIBERNIA

"HIBERNIA"

Marples, William
and Sons
Sheffield

Martin Brothers
and Company
Sheffield

Martin, Hall
and Company
Shrewsbury Works
Sheffield

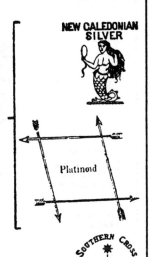

NEW CALEDONIAN
SILVER

Platinoid

Martino, F. R.
Birmingham

Mason Brothers,
Ltd.
London

SOUTHERN CROSS

BRAND

Mather, William
Manchester

Maw, S., Son,
and Thompson
London

Meriden Britannia
Company
London

Merzbach, Lang
and Fellheimer
London

Meyerstein,
William
and Company
London

Milner, William
and Sons
Leek

Moenich, Oscar
and Company
London

Mordan, S.
and Company
London

Moreton, John
and Company
*Wolverhampton,
Sheffield
and London*

Morton, John
and Company
*Sheffield
and London*

Morton, W.
Sheffield

Muir, H. B.
and Company
London

1847—ROGERS BROS.—A 1

THE "NEEDLE"

S. MORDAN & Cº

EMPRESS

BUTTERFLY

J. M. & Cº.

H.B. MUIR & Cº
LONDON

Muirhead, James
and Company
Glasgow

Neal, John
and Company
London

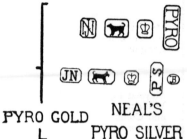

PYRO GOLD   NEAL'S
        PYRO SILVER

Needham, J.
Sheffield

Needham, Veall,
and Tyzack
Eye Witness Works
Sheffield

Neill, Sharman
Dermott
Belfast

Newton, Ellis
Birmingham

Newton, Francis
and Sons
Portobello Works
Sheffield

Newton, Frederick
and Company
London

Nodder, John
and Son
Sheffield

North, J.
Sheffield

Nowill, John
and Sons
Sheffield

O'Connor, Patrick
Lancashire

Openshaw
and Company
*Birmingham
and London*

Osborn and Elliott
Sheffield

Oxley, John
Sheffield

Padley, Parkin
and Company
Sheffield

Padley, William
and Son
Sheffield

Page, William
and Company
Birmingham

Parkin
and Marshall
Telegraph Works
Sheffield

XL ALL

P & M   WP

Padley, Staniforth
and Company
Sheffield

P S
& C°

Payton
and Company
Birmingham

Pears, A. and F.
*London
and Middlesex*

Perry and
Company, Ltd.
Birmingham

Phosphor Bronze
Company, The
Southwark Surrey

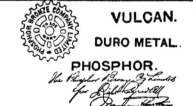

VULCAN.

DURO METAL.

PHOSPHOR.

Pinder, James
and Company
Colonial Plate
Works
Sheffield

Piston Freezing
Machine and Ice
Company, The
Middlesex

Piston Freezing Machine
and Ice Company.

Planters' Stores and
Agency Company
London

Platnauer Brothers
Bristol

Potosi,
The Company
Birmingham

ELECTRO-POTOSI

POTOSI SILVER

Potter, John Henry
Sheffield

SILVA

Prime, Thomas
and Son
Birmingham

Reading, N. C.
and Company
Birmingham
(continued)

Reid, George
and Company
London

Pringle, Robert
and Company
Wilderness Works
Middlesex

Rhodes Brothers
Sheffield

Pryor, Tzack
and Company
Sheffield

Rhodes, Jehoiada
Alsop
Britain Works
Sheffield

Rabone Brothers
and Company
Birmingham

RABONE

RABONE BROTHERS & Cº

Richards,
Theophilus
and Company
Birmingham

THEOPHILUS RICHARDS & Co.

Rae, William
and Company
Liverpool

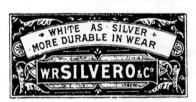

Richards, Thomas
Spendelow
and Company
Birmingham

Ramsbottom,
Walter J.
Vine Works
Sheffield

Richardson,
Richard
Cornwall Works
Sheffield

Ridal, John
Paxton Works
Sheffield

RAINBOW

Reading, N. C.
and Company
Birmingham

Ridge, Joseph
Sheffield

Ridge, Woodcock
and Hardy
Sheffield

Roberts and Belk
Furnival Works
Sheffield

SYLFERET.

Rodgers, Joseph
and Sons
Sheffield

Roberts and Briggs
Sheffield

Roberts and Hall
Sheffield

Roberts, J.
Sheffield

Roberts and Slater
Sheffield

Robinson
and Company
Sheffield

Robinson,
Higginson
Liverpool

J RODGERS
& SONS

Nº 6
NORFOLK
STREET
SHEFFIELD

JOSEPH RODGERS & SONS
CUTLERS TO THEIR MAJESTIES
Nº 6 NORFOLK STREET
SHEFFIELD

V R
JOSEPH RODGERS & SONS
CUTLERS TO HER MAJESTY.

JOSEPH RODGERS

RODGERS
CUTLERS
TO HER
MAJESTY

Rodgers, Joseph
and Sons
Sheffield

RODGERS'   ORIGINAL & GENUINE PLATE

RODGERSINE

Rodgers, Joseph
and Sons
Sheffield
(continued)

JOSEPH RODGERS & SONS

RODGERS

Rogers, Henry
Sons and
Company
*Sheffield and
Wolverhampton*

Rosing Brothers
and Company
London

Rossell, Henry
and Company
Sheffield

Round, John
and Son, Ltd.
Tudor Works
and
Arundel Works
Sheffield

VALARIUM

KENDULAM

Rowe, Charles
Courtney
Middlesex

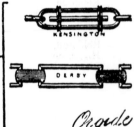

Royle, T.
Sheffield

Ryland, William
Gatefield Works
Sheffield

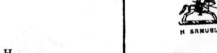

Samuel, H.
and Sons
Manchester

Sansom and
Creswick
Sheffield

Sansom and
Davenport
Sheffield

Savage, W. S.
and Company
Sheffield

Schürhoff, H.
and Company
Birmingham

Selig, Sonnenthal
and Company
London

Shaw, John
and Sons, Ltd.
Wolverton

Shaw and Fisher
Sheffield

Sherwood, John
and Sons
Birmingham

Shoolbred, James
and Company
Middlesex

Silber and
Fleming, Ltd.
London

Silverston, Isaac
and Company
Birmingham

Sissons, William
and George
*Sheffield
and London*

Skidmore, W.
Enema Works
Sheffield

Slack Brothers
Leicester Works
Sheffield

Slack and Grinold
Bath Works
Sheffield

Slater Brothers
Sheffield

Slater, J. and Son
Sheffield

Slater, Son
and Horton
Sheffield

Smith, Charles
Sheffield

Stacey, Henry
and Horton
Sheffield

Staniforth, William
Thomas
Ascend Works
Sheffield

Smith, Josephus
Sheffield

Societe Anonyme
des Couverts
Alfenide
Paris

J.S

ALFE
NIDE

Steam
Electro-Plating
and Gilding
Company, The
Southampton

Sorby, Robert
and Sons
Sheffield

KANGAROO

Stratford,
W. and H.
Sheffield

Swann and Adams
Canada Works
Birmingham

MIXITINE

Hay, William
Birmingham

Spencer, Matthias
and Sons
Sheffield

Albion Steel Works
Sheffield

MATTHIAS SPENCER & SONS

Taylor Brothers
Adelaide Works
Sheffield

Taylor and
Company
Swansea

Speyer, C. A. E.
and Company
London

HERALD

TRUMPETER

Teasdell, G.
London

GT

Thompson
and Brown
Sheffield

T&B

Thompson, J.
Sheffield

JT

Speyer, Schwerdt
and Company
London

Thornhill, Walter
Middlesex

Spurrier and
Company
London

GORDON SILVER

Tidmarsh, James
London

MEXICAN SILVER

JTMI 3

Timm, F. E.
Sheffield

Townsend,
Francis John
Sheffield

LIFE

Stacey Brothers
Sheffield

Charlasting

Towndrow Brothers
Sheffield

Turner, Thomas
Sheffield

Turner, Thomas
and Company
Suffolk Works
Sheffield

Unite, G.
Birmingham

Van Wart, Son
and Company
Birmingham

Vernon, James
and Brother
Wigtown

Vernon's Patent
China and Glass
Company, Ltd.
London

Vivian, H. H. and
Company, Ltd.
Birmingham

von der Meden,
Carl August
London

Walker and Hall
Sheffield

Walker, Knowles
and Company
Sheffield

Walsham, R. and J.
Birmingham

Walton, G. E. and
Company, Ltd.
Birmingham

Ward, George
Sheffield

Ward, W. and S.
Manchester

Waterhouse,
George and
Company
Sheffield

Wells, Gallimore
and Taylor
Birmingham

Wheeler, George
Birmingham

White, Henderson
and Company
Elcho Works
Sheffield

White
and Johnstone
Sheffield

White and Ridsdale
London

White, Thomas
Birmingham

Whitehouse,
Frederick
Lion Works
Birmingham

Imperial
F.W.

Electro-Imperial.
F.W.

Imperial Silver
F.W.

Whiteley, William
Middlesex

UNIVERSAL PROVIDER.

Wilkin, George
Palmerston Works
Sheffield

Wilkinson, Henry
and Company, Ltd.
Sheffield

Wilkinson, T.
and Sons
Birmingham

Williamson, Henry
London

ACME.

Wilson, John
Sheffield

Wilson and Davis
*London
and Sheffield*

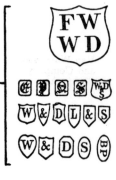

Winter, Robert
Sheffield

2216

Woolley, James,
Sons and Company
Manchester

BOVAL

Wostenholm,
George and
Son, Ltd.
Washington Works
Sheffield

I. XL

Wostenholme, J.
Sheffield

J.W.

Wostenholme,
W. F.
Sheffield

W.F.W.

Yates, John
and Sons
Birmingham

Y & S

J Y & S

YATES & SONS

J. YATES & SONS

JOHN YATES & SONS

YATES
VIRGINIAN SILVER

Y

V S

Yates, John
and Sons
Birmingham
(continued)

YATES'S
VIRGINIAN

York, Samuel
and Company
Wolverhampton

Glossary

Acanthus: a form of ornamentation taken from the acanthus leaf, originally used on the Corinthian capital.

Alcomy: an alloy of various base metals, principally used in button making.

Alloy: a substance composed of two or more metals intimately united, usually intermixed when molten.

Apprentice: one who is bound by indentures to serve another person with a view to learning a trade.

Argentine: an alloy of tin and antimony used as plated metal.

Argyle: a container for serving sauces, originally introduced in silver, constructed with an inner jacket to hold hot water to preserve the heat of the gravy.

Assay: a chemical test to determine the quantity of one or more ingredients in a substance.

Base Metal: an alloy or metal of comparatively low value to which a coating or plating is normally applied.

Bell Metal: a variety of Sheffield Plate consisting of an unusually heavy coating of silver, introduced in 1789 by Samuel Roberts.

Biggin-time: the term applied to a refreshment period during which coffee was served from a biggin.

Bleeding: the technical term applied to pieces of plate whereon the copper base is exposed.

Bobeche: a saucer-shaped dish to catch the drippings of the candle.

Britannia Metal: a silver-white alloy of tin, antimony and copper, sometimes containing zinc and bismuth.

Buffing: polishing by the use of a mechanical wheel equipped with a soft mop.

Burnish: to make shiny or lustrous.

Café au lait Pots: the term applied to side-handled coffee dispensers from which hot milk and coffee are poured simultaneously.

Chamberstick: a container for a candle used primarily as a lighting device in a bedroom.

Chasing: process of ornamenting metal by means of tools such as a hammer and chisel.

Christie's: one of London's oldest and most famous auction rooms specializing in the disposal of works of art.

Ciborium: a goblet-shaped vessel in which the Eucharistic wafers are kept.

Coat of Arms: the heraldic escutcheon assigned to a family.

Condiment: a pungent substance used to give relish for food, a spice.

Cutler: one who makes, deals in, or repairs eating utensils or knives.

Date Letter: the insigne assigned by the London Goldsmiths Company to denote the particular year in which a piece of solid silver is produced.

Dish Cross: an article made in silver or plate used to support a porcelain bowl or dish ring, sometimes equipped with an alcohol lamp.

Dish Ring: originally of Irish descent. It is a circular, pierced holder for a wooden or porcelain bowl. Sometimes referred to as a potato ring.

Domestic Plate—the term applied to silver used in the home as opposed to that used in the service of the church.

Doublé: a French term used to designate silver plated ware.

Electrolysis: the process of conduction of an electric current by an electrolyte of charged particles.

Electroplate: the term applied to articles consisting of a base metal coated with silver made by the process of electrolysis.

Embossing: the raising in relief from a surface of any ornament by mechanical means.

Epergne: a centerpiece of French extraction usually consisting of a center dish surrounded by smaller dishes.

Flagon: a vessel for liquors, normally equipped with a lid and spout.

Flame: the term applied to a removable decoration used to replace a candle, normally in the center of a candelabra.

Folding Biscuit Box: a container introduced during the Victorian period for the accommodation and service of hot muffins. Consisting of two opening sides fitted with screens and equipped with a center handle.

Fluted: a type of grooving.

Forged Marks: the term applied to hallmarks that have been fraudulently stamped on a piece of silver.

Freeman: a member of a corporation, possessing certain privileges.

Fusion: act or operation of melting, as the fusion of metals. Usually accomplished by the application of intense heat.

Gadroon: an ornamentation produced by notching or carving a rounded surface.

Galvanic Battery: a type of battery named after Luigi Galvani wherein direct currents of electricity are used.

German Silver: a silver-white alloy consisting essentially of copper, zinc, and nickel. In modern times referred to as nickel silver.

Gold Plating: the covering of an article with gold.

Goldsmiths Company: the organization under whose jurisdiction and regulation the silver industry has been conducted.

Hallmark: the official mark of the Goldsmiths Company used on articles of gold and silver to indicate their genuineness.

Imperial Measure: a term used in Great Britain to designate the legal standard weights and measures.

Katé: a Malayan word used to denote a measure by which tea was sold.

Kilo: a prefix, used in the metric system, meaning *thousand*.

King's Head: a mark applied on a piece of silver to denote payment of a tax assessed by the Crown.

Mace: an emblem of authority normally associated with English Parliamentary procedure.

Maker's Mark: the term applied to the insigne struck on a piece of silver or plate to denote the person responsible for the production of the article.

Malleable: capable of being extended or shaped by beating with a hammer, ductile.

Marrow Scoop: a long, narrow silver implement with a scoop center used to extract marrow from a bone.

Metalsmith: one versed in the intricacies of working with metals.

Monteith: the term applied to a particular type of punch bowl made with a serrated edge. Its origin is traced to the Earl of Monteith.

Motif: a salient feature of the composition of a work.

Mount: a decorative border.

Nozzle: a socket for a candlestick.

Ormolu: a variety of brass or bronze mixed with ground gold to simulate gold in appearance.

Paten: a dish of precious metal used in the Eucharistic service.

Patina: mellow appearance of surface, usually due to age of article.

Peg Tankard: a container for ale or beer with inner notches for measuring a drink.

Piercing: openwork decoration.

Pinchbeck: an alloy of copper or zinc used to imitate gold.

Pipkin: a container for sauce, usually with a protruding handle at right angles.

Pit Marks: minute holes usually found on lead or soft metal borders.

Pix Box: a small container used in Church Service. The Host is carried in it.

Plaqué: a French term used to denote the thickness of plating.

Plateau: an ornamental flat dish equipped with a mirror, generally used under an epergne or centerpiece.

Plating Vat: the tank in which silver plated ware is subjected to electrolysis.

Revolving Tureen: a container with a roll cover and hot water compartment introduced during the Victorian Era.

Rococo: a style of extravagant ornamentation developed in France during the Louis XV period.

Royal Patronage: the encouragement of the Royal Family as applied to trade.

Serrated: notched.

Sheffield Plate: the term given to plated articles made by the process of fusion.

Silver Edge: an ornamental border of solid silver constituency.

Silver Shield: the term applied to an insertion of solid silver on plate to hold engraving.

Snuffer: an extinguisher for a flame.

Solid Silver: metal of the constituency of .925 of silver and .025 of alloy.

Soy Stand: a cruet or condiment holder.

Swaged: shaped by the process of rolling or hammering.

Syphon Stand: a pierced holder for a seltzer water bottle.

Tinning: the act of working with tin, as tin plating.

Town Mark: the insigne assigned to a city and applied as a hallmark to denote the locale of manufacture.

Trowel: a spade-shaped instrument, frequently made in silver and suitably engraved, as upon the laying of a cornerstone.

Victorian Plate: silver plated ware made during the period c.1840–1900, by the process of electrolysis.

Winchester Measure: a system of measures formerly recorded in Winchester, medieval capital of England. Early silver and silver plate drinking vessels were made according to Winchester Measures.

Wine Cistern: a large vat or tank for holding vintage drinks, normally used only at large functions.

Wine Funnel: a silver article with strainer and oilcan spout for decanting wine.

Wine Taster: a small receptacle used by professional tasters at wineries to judge flavor and quality.

Index